Mike Ferguson

Poems
in your Pocket

Imaginative Approaches
to GCSE Poetry

Pearson Education Limited
Edinburgh Gate
Harlow
Essex
CM20 2JE

England and Associated Companies throughout the World

ISBN 0-582-41989-1

First published 1999

Printed in Italy by G. Canale & C. S.p.A.

Contents

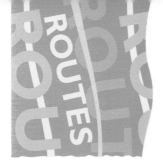

Introduction

Poetry is everywhere. You may feel that you don't know much about it, but poetry has in fact been an important part of your life and will continue to be so long after you have finished studying it for, amongst other things, your GCSE!

- Poetry is in the song lyrics you sing now and in the nursery rhymes you had read to you as a child and perhaps memorised.
- Poetry is in the football chants you shout at the top of your voice from the terraces.
- Poetry is in the language of advertising you see on television, billboards and in magazines, as well as the jingles you hear on radio.

You will have read a variety of poems at school and perhaps had a visiting poet to read and run writing workshops. Hopefully, you will have enjoyed much of this and begun to read poetry for pleasure as well as study it in some depth, learning why and how writers express themselves in poems.

When you study poetry, your understanding and appreciation will be informed by these familiar and common features. However, to gain the maximum enjoyment and insight you also need to have experience of reading a range of poems and to develop the critical skills that help you express your understanding convincingly and with sensitivity. Being able to write well about poetry isn't a skill just for GCSE coursework and examinations – being able to communicate thoughts and feelings with clarity and supporting detail helps you to consolidate these ideas for yourself and increase confidence in your personal interpretation of poems.

The study of poetry is an important element in GCSE English and English Literature, and you will be required to read widely and respond to this either in written course-work or examinations. You will demonstrate your understanding and appreciation by being able to cover the skills required by the GCSE syllabuses. These are called *assessment objectives* and are common to all of the syllabuses. You will need to demonstrate your ability to:

- read and respond critically, sensitively and with insight and engagement (for example, your personal appreciation is as important as your critical understanding)
- select and make appropriate reference to textual evidence (for example, choosing relevant lines to quote from a poem)
- develop and sustain interpretation, as well as recognise alternative interpretations
- explore how language, structure and forms contribute to the meaning of texts (for example, why a poem is written in colloquial language or in the sonnet form)
- explore relationships and comparisons within and between texts
- show understanding of literary tradition (for example, when, why and by whom a poem was written)
- show appreciation of social and historical influences (for example, the differing views about war expressed by Shakespeare or First World War poets)

- comment on the ways language varies and changes (for example, the difference between the language of British and American poets or between nineteenth- and twentieth-century poets).

How this book will help you

Poems from around the world and from Shakespeare to the present day are included in this book for you to read and explore. They cover such diverse subjects as playing football, war and unwanted teenage pregnancies, and are presented in tones ranging from ecstatic to despairing. The writing of poetry is often the most powerful means of expressing personal feelings and experiences. This in itself can make poems engaging and important to read, but what makes this memorable and moving is the way we can so often relate to these feelings and experiences.

Writing of poetry is not always easy. The idea that creative inspiration suddenly appears as if out of thin air is a myth. Most poets would acknowledge that they have to put considerable effort and discipline into their writing, and these aspects, along with flair and inspiration, produce the most memorable and meaningful work. This being the case, it seems reasonable to acknowledge that some effort and discipline in the study of poetry on the part of the reader is equally important. When you are required to write or talk about poetry, there are skills you need to help you do this successfully.

Poems in Your Pocket aims to give you the skills with which to convey your personal response as well as relate this to the poet's message and methods. You will explore the feelings that motivate poets to express themselves, and examine the writing tools of their trade. In doing this, you should find yourself relating closely to many of the experiences described and reacting strongly to many of the opinions, thoughts and feelings expressed. Hopefully, you will also learn to appreciate the powerful effects of the way language is used and the shaping of this in various forms.

How to work through this book

By working through the first three chapters and being introduced to the key elements of Tones, Techniques and Types – **the Three Ts** – you will embrace the obvious features of reading and responding to poetry. This should provide a compact and coherent means by which you can, with some ease, approach the study of poetry. The Three Ts is a mnemonic – a device to aid memory – and can be easily retained. It is especially important that you retain such a framework when responding to the study of poetry in, amongst other areas, either GCSE coursework assignments or examinations.

The first three chapters are therefore structured to provide a clear route to the reading, appreciation and study of poetry:

- **Chapter 1 Tones** provides a general introduction and focuses on the first stage of a reader's understanding of a poem which is recognising and being able to describe its tone. A Tones Checklist is provided to give you a structure for identifying and examining those features of poetry that suggest mood and feeling. The work in this chapter will provide you with opportunities to *explore relationships within and between texts*. The examination of particular poems will help you to *recognise alternative interpretations*.

- **Chapter 2 Techniques** provides a snapshot of the obvious and common poetic techniques and reminds you (and teachers!) that once a poetic technique has been identified, it needs to be supported by comment on its purpose and effect. A Techniques Checklist is provided.

  With the study of poetry a key element of GCSE English and English Literature, it is particularly important to stress the dangers of the t-spotter – those who can describe the make and name of a train, but have no appreciation for the lives of the passengers inside. Identification of techniques will be rewarded, but it is an explanation and then exploration of their purpose and effect on the reader that will gain the highest marks. For example, the use of alliteration in poetry is often spotted by students, but with little reference to its purpose and effect. Commenting on the particular impact of the sound effects created will demonstrate an exploration of the use of this technique. The work in this chapter will provide you with opportunities to *explore how language and structure contribute to the meaning of texts* as well as examine the *ways in which language varies and changes*.

- **Chapter 3 Types** provides a general introduction to the use of rhyme and rhythm and how these are an integral part of most traditional poetic forms. The sonnet is given extended coverage, and a range of free verse forms are explored in contrast. The work in this chapter will provide you with opportunities to *explore how structure and forms contribute to the meaning of texts*. It will also help you to gain an *understanding of literary tradition* and how *social and historical influences* can determine the language and form of poems. The chapter includes a Types Checklist.

  Your teacher will be able to give you worksheets providing many creative and analytical opportunities to explore forms further.

The following three chapters are structured to provide a clear route to writing about the poetry you have read and studied:

- **Chapter 4 Annotating poetry** gives practical guidance on how to make notes about poetry on the page and as accompanying keyed annotations. Many GCSE syllabuses provide anthologies of poems for study and you will be encouraged to make notes on these copies. It is important that such annotations are not overdone and that you write these to help you retain and present a fresh and lively appreciation of the poems rather than a rehearsed and therefore much less engaging response. This chapter will provide you with opportunities to *select and make appropriate reference to textual evidence*.

- **Chapter 5 Companion poems** offers considerable material and guidance on the detailed comparison of poems which is a key requirement of GCSE English and English Literature. This will provide you with useful practice for writing in examinations or ideas for coursework assignments. This chapter will provide you with opportunities to *read and respond critically, sensitively and with insight and engagement*. You will be encouraged to *explore relationships and comparisons within and between texts and to develop and sustain interpretation*. This will be closely linked to how *language, structure and form contribute to the meaning of texts*.

- **Chapter 6 Examining poetry** offers advice on how to plan, structure and write essays both for coursework and examinations. This includes references to sample student answers and guidance on exam techniques.

The **Glossary** gives you definitions of and examples for technical terms. This will help you in your reading of the book as well as provide you with a critical vocabulary to use once you have the confidence to appreciate and talk about the purpose and effect of poetical techniques.

Your reading and responding to the poetry in this book is therefore carefully guided. Whether studying independently or in a class, by working through each chapter you will move towards an overall understanding and appreciation of how poetry presents its meanings and messages. Within each chapter there are *Thinking, Discussion* and *Writing* tasks which help you to develop the skills necessary to read and respond to poetry. There are also occasional oral and creative writing *Activities* to support these tasks.

In your pocket

Whilst *Poems in Your Pocket* aims to provide you with the skills needed to read and respond to poetry for GCSE coursework and examinations, as well as before and after this significant moment, the selection and presentation of poems reflects a genuine attempt to engage and interest you. The choice of poems meets the requirements of the National Curriculum, but there is also a commitment to present poetry that will tap into your own experiences and offer a range of voices that are demanding, enriching, stimulating and sometimes very familiar.

This book will not literally fit into your pocket! However, it is hoped that you will gain considerable enjoyment and skill from reading and studying the poems in it. These are the qualities that you can then carry around in your pocket to pull out and help at any time and in any situation where you are engaging with poetry. Dip in and see what you can discover...

Tones

When you can hear a poet's 'tone of voice', you have identified the tone of a poem and solved the most important clue to its meaning. Actual spoken words in a poem make it easier to recognise a distinctive voice or voices. If the poet is mocking or questioning these voices, however, this could change the overall tone of a poem. Sometimes, it takes careful reading and re-reading of a poem before you can hear the poet's feelings. Even when the poet speaks directly to you as reader, you will have to listen for clues to help you to identify the overall tone. A poet's unique use of language and the presentation of the poem on the page combine to express particular feelings.

Read Maya Angelou's poem, 'Life Doesn't Frighten Me'. The first reading of a poem is always done so that you can simply take in the story and, hopefully, enjoy it.

Life Doesn't Frighten Me

Shadows on the wall
Noises down the hall
Life doesn't frighten me at all
Bad dogs barking loud
5 Big ghosts in a cloud
Life doesn't frighten me at all.

Mean old Mother Goose
Lions on the loose
They don't frighten me at all
10 Dragons breathing flame
On my counterpane
That doesn't frighten me at all.

I go boo
Make them shoo
15 I make fun
Way them run
I won't cry
So they fly
I just smile
20 They go wild
Life doesn't frighten me at all.

Tough guys in a fight
All alone at night
Life doesn't frighten me at all.
25 Panthers in the park
Strangers in the dark
No, they don't frighten me at all.

That new classroom where
Boys all pull my hair
30 (Kissy little girls
With their hair in curls)
They don't frighten me at all.

Don't show me frogs and snakes
And listen for my scream.
35 If I'm afraid at all
It's only in my dreams.

I've got a magic charm
That I keep up my sleeve,
I can walk the ocean floor
40 And never have to breathe.

Life doesn't frighten me at all
Not at all
Not at all
Life doesn't frighten me at all.

Maya Angelou

Read her poem a second time and this time concentrate on the speaker. Listen carefully to the thoughts and feelings she is expressing. Ask yourself whether the poet sounds confident or anxious. It isn't as clear cut as it might at first appear!

Tones checklist

When searching for tone, listen for these clues:

Voice
- Does the speaker talk directly to you, the reader?
- Is the speaker reporting someone else's thoughts?
- How reliable would you say their judgment is?

Language
- What kind of words does the poet use? e.g. are they everyday, old-fashioned, conversational, descriptive, simple, difficult?
- What impact do they have?

Content
- Which details are mentioned?
- What picture is built up?
- If something is missed out, is it significant?

Sound
- What sorts of sounds can be heard? What sound qualities do the consonants and the vowels have? e.g. are they long, or short? Hard or soft?
- Are any sounds emphasised or repeated? Do any fade out?
- Is there a rhyme pattern? What effect does this have?

Structure
- How are the words presented on the page?
- How long are the lines?
- Are there stanzas?
- What is the effect of the structure?

Searching for a tone

Note how positive the tone of Maya Angelou's poem is. It appears defiant. If, as a simple starter, you can decide whether a poem is either positive or negative you can then move on to more precise definitions of its tone. If you believe the tone is positive/supportive, you would be thinking of confident, hopeful, and enthusiastic feelings. If you find the tone negative/critical, you would be thinking of anxious, pessimistic and uncertain feelings.

Use the Tones Checklist to focus your search for the tone of this poem. Write down your answers to the questions on the following page. Each question is followed by one piece of evidence from the poem to help you with the task.

Thinking and writing

1 In Maya Angelou's poem, is the poet speaking directly to the reader? (The words 'I' and 'me' appear throughout the poem.)

2 Do the language and content give any clues to the speaker? (The language of 'I go boo' and the reference to 'Mean old Mother Goose' suggest the age of the speaker.)

3 Do the sounds in the poem help us? (The **rhymes** 'boo/shoo', 'fun/run' and 'fly/my' are simple and childlike.)

4 Do the structure and presentation give us any clues? (The 'chorus' line 'Life doesn't frighten me at all' is repeated so often it begins to sound as if the poet is convincing herself.)

5 At this stage you should try two different readings aloud of the poem: once in a childlike and anxious voice and then again in an adult and confident voice. Which reading do you feel is the more realistic and why?

6 Do your readings of the poem and your answers to the above questions make you want to change the earlier suggestion that this is a positive poem?

7 Write a list of the words you would now use to describe the tone of Angelou's poem.

Tone words

Before exploring more poems and their tones, it would be useful to look at ways of developing a vocabulary to describe the subtle shades of tone in a poem.

Consider some of the following words. It is not a complete list, but it is a start …

angry	sad	mischievous
defeated	weary	celebratory
upbeat	sarcastic	ironic
happy	despairing	satirical
conspiratorial	triumphant	indifferent
ambiguous	romantic	argumentative
cheeky	casual	nostalgic
aggressive	meditative	defiant

Activities

● One person chooses a tone word from the above list and acts it out for the rest of the group or class who then try to guess which it is.

● Many of these words could be paired or put together in clusters of similar meaning. Copy the following table. Take the words from the list above and place them into two categories:

Positive/Supportive	Negative/Critical
upbeat	*weary*

Compare your lists. Have you noticed more words in one list compared with the other? Are there any major disagreements over certain words? If it has been difficult to place some words, can you explain the reasons? Can you think of any other categories that might be needed?

Add three more words to each of the categories you have decided upon.

Exploring tones

The following groups of poems display a variety of tones. The tasks based on them ask you to identify and then think about the purpose and effect of the poets' tone of voice.

Views on childhood

While Angelou's poem could be seen as hopeful, defiant or nervous, Moniza Alvi's poem, 'Indian Cooking', seems to be a happy celebration and reflection. The poem paints a simple but realistic picture of cooking a meal and how this experience reminds the poet of her family.

Indian Cooking

The bottom of the pan was a palette —
paprika, cayenne, dhania
haldi, heaped like powder-paints.

Melted ghee made lakes, golden rivers.
5   The keema frying, my mother waited
for the fat to bubble to the surface.

Friends brought silver-leaf.
I dropped it on khir —
special rice pudding for parties.

10   I tasted the landscape, customs
of my father's country —
its fever on biting a chilli.

Moniza Alvi

Thinking and writing

1   Compare 'Indian Cooking' with Angelou's poem. Use the Tones Checklist (on page 11) to help you and remember to look closely at the language used in 'Indian Cooking'.

2   Can you determine the tone more easily in one poem than in the other? Write a couple of sentences on any similarities or differences in tone.

Violence

The content of a poem can provide clues to tone. Although the next pair of poems are different in their subject matter, they express equally strong feelings. In each poem, the poet adopts the voice of an imagined character – or **persona** – in order to make their points.

War is a subject that arouses strong feelings and emotions. War poetry can be very moving to read because it captures the horror or even the elation of fighting. In 'Base Details', Siegfried Sassoon blames uncaring army officers for sending young soldiers to their deaths in the First World War.

Base Details

If I were fierce, and bald, and short of breath,
I'd live with scarlet Majors at the Base,
And speed glum heroes up the line to death.
You'd see me with my puffy petulant face,
5 Guzzling and gulping in the best hotel,
Reading the Roll of Honour. 'Poor young chap,'
I'd say – 'I used to know his father well;
Yes, we've lost heavily in this last scrap.'
And when the war is done and youth stone dead,
10 I'd toddle safely home and die – in bed.

Siegfried Sassoon

Thinking and writing

1 Sassoon begins his poem 'Base Details' with the important word 'If'. Why is this so important to the whole poem?

2 Make a list of the negative words and phrases he uses to describe and paint a very visual picture of being an army officer (e.g. 'fierce' and 'bald').

3 This poem gives us the direct 'voice' of the Major. Imagine you were a young soldier overhearing this. Write a sentence to say how you would feel.

4 Comment on the contrast between the phrases 'youth stone dead' and 'toddle safely home'.

5 What words would best sum up the tone of this poem?

A more modern but equally aggressive poem, in terms of its tone, is Anne Rouse's 'England Nil'. This poem also adopts a voice. As in 'Base Details', where Sassoon becomes one of the English officers he despises, in 'England Nil' Rouse becomes one of the English football 'supporters' she criticises.

The advance to Hamburg broke with all the plans.
Doug spelled them out in Luton Friday night.
Someone had ballsed it up. A dozen vans
Waited in convoy, ringside. Blue and white
5   We stumbled through. The beer
When we found it in that piss-hole of jerries
Was all we needed. Who won the war,
Anyway? Who nuked Dresden? Two fairies
Skittered behind the bar, talking Kraut
10   Or maybe Arabic. We clocked the poison
Smiles and chanted till the SS threw us out.
Stuttgart was a tea-party to this. One
By one they've nicked us, berserk with fear.
You've been Englished but you won't forget it, never.

Anne Rouse

Thinking and writing

1   Using the same method as Sassoon, in 'England Nil' Rouse becomes the person she is criticising by adopting the voice of an English football hooligan. List the negative words and phrases used to paint the scene and the tone.

2   Pick out two examples of the most obviously nasty language and comment on how this is used to expose and criticise the 'supporters'.

3   The voice in the poem is made to sound victorious and triumphant. How do we know that Rouse wants us to reject this tone?

Relationships

The following group of four poems all present varying tones of voice and messages. They are linked by expressing strong opinions on serious subjects. Read each poem carefully, before completing the tasks on page 20. As you read each poem for the first time, try to follow its story. Each poem describes a single event or a series of events. Heaney's poem, for example, was written after his mother's death and describes a simple but important moment he once spent with her.

Latitudes

In Palermo, six-year-old Paulo feels
the crossed lines stung into his back
for taking one orange from his father's orchard.

In Abadan, Hanah is playing in a sun-parched field.
5   She steps on a landmine – for one eternal instant
sees all the roofs of her village.

Raj is twelve, born in Karachi. Polio, no parents,
he is quicksilver among the boots of tourists
on his two wheels.

10   North London – two brothers drugged with telly,
lashed all day by dad's brute tongue: followers
of the glue and the brown-paper bag.

Galway Bay – the Gardai gather awkwardly
round the bloated marbled doll, the fifteen-year-old
15   mother, both face-down, rocked by the waves.

All the while, in a New York apartment
a woman plays Mozart through a stethoscope
to her unborn child.

Mario Petrucci

Class, this is Fatima
all the way from –
who can spell Bosnia for me?

I know if she could speak
5   English, she would tell us
what a lucky girl she feels
to be here in Bromley – THIS IS BROMLEY –
while all her friends
had to stay behind in –
10   who can spell Sarajevo for me?

This morning we are going to carry on
with our Nativity Play For Today.
Fatima has lovely blonde hair – HAIR –
so she is going to play the Virgin Mary;
15   then she won't have to say anything.
No sulking. Lisa; you can be
the landlady. She's got a nice rude speech
and a shiny handbag.

Alex is Joseph; you other boys
20   are soldiers. But remember
you're not to get carried away
killing the babies. This is acting.

Fatima, sit here, dear;
this is your baby – BABY.
25   Joseph, put your hand on her shoulder.
Now, angel chorus, let's have the first verse
of 'Hope for the world, peace evermore.'
Herod, stop fidgeting with your kalashnikov.
Fatima, why are you crying?

Carole Satyamurti

Clearances

When all the others were away at Mass
I was all hers as we peeled potatoes.
They broke the silence, let fall one by one
Like solder weeping off the soldering iron:
5   Cold comforts set between us, things to share
Gleaming in a bucket of clean water.
And again let fall. Little pleasant splashes
From each other's work would bring us to our senses.

So while the parish priest at her bedside
10   Went hammer and tongs at the prayers for
    the dying
And some were responding and some crying
I remembered her head bent towards my head,
Her breath in mine, our fluent dipping knives –
Never closer the whole rest of our lives.

Seamus Heaney

for Rita *with* Love

You come home from school
on a special bus
full of people
who look like you
5   and love like you
and you met me
for the first time
and you loved me.
You love everybody
10 so much that it's not safe
to let you out alone.
Eleven years of love
and trust and time for you to learn
that you can't go on loving like this.
15 Unless you are stopped
you will embrace every person you see.
Normal people don't do that.
Some Normal people will hurt you
very badly because you do.

20 Cripples don't look nice
but you embrace them.
You kissed a wino on the bus
and he broke down and cried
and he said 'Nobody has kissed me

25 for the last 30 years.
But you did.
You touched my face
with your fingers and said
"I like you".'
30 The world will never
be ready for you.
Your way is right
and the world will
never be ready.

35 We could learn everything
that we need to know
by watching you
going to your special school
in your special bus
40 full of people
who look like you
and love like you
and it's not safe
to let you out alone.
45 If you're not normal
there is very little hope
for the rest of us.

Pat Ingoldsby

Thinking and writing

1 Copy and complete the grid below, which is based on the Tones Checklist.

2 Then create a set of questions for each poem that would help another reader to comment on their tone. Their answers will need to include some supporting evidence.

	Voice	**Language**	**Content**	**Sound**	**Structure**
Latitudes			children in the world who suffer		
Fatima	teacher speaking to her/his class				
Clearances				rhyme of 'knives'/'lives' at end adds conclusion	a sonnet: last two lines draw a solemn close
For Rita With Love		simple language spoken by adult – why?			

The female of the species

One way to practise differentiating tones in poems is to look at a selection all written on the same theme. This requires a little more fine-tuning than noticing the differences in poems with varying themes. It will also test your vocabulary of tone words and encourage you to extend it.

The following seven poems are all concerned with representations of women or the role of women. As you read the poems, listen for their 'tone of voice' and make notes about tone. Start by asking yourself whether they are negative or positive in their overall presentation of women. To develop these first thoughts, apply the Tones Checklist (on page 11).

the Woman who keeps her Breasts in the Back Garden

Why do you keep your breasts in the back garden?
Well – it's a male-dominated society, isn't it?
Yes, I know it is, but could you explain . . . ?
Certainly I'll explain, certainly:
5 Seeing as how it's a male-dominated society
And there is all this ballyhoo about breasts,
  I decided to keep my pair of breasts in the back garden
And once or twice a day I take them out for a walk –
Usually on a leash but sometimes I unleash them –
10 And they jump up and down and prance a bit
And in that way the males can get their bosom-gaping done with
And I can get on with my other activities.
I used to leave them out at night under the glorious stars
But then little men started coming in over the walls.
15 I have other things on my mind besides my breasts:
Australia – for example – Australia.
To tell you the truth, I think a great deal about Australia.
Thank you very much for talking to us, Miss Delia Fair.

Paul Durcan

She Is Not
Afraid of
Burglars

It's lunchtime
and he's training the dog again.
He says to the dog in a cross voice,
'Stay there.'
5   The dog obeys him.

When he goes home
he forgets to leave the cross voice
in the green where he trains his dog
and spits out unwoven troubles
10   that won't fit in his head.

He says to his wife,
'Stay there.'
His wife obeys him.
She sees how good he is with the dog
15   and how the dog obeys his cross voice.

She boasts to the locals,
'I would never be afraid of burglars
with my husband in the house.'

The locals, busting for news, ask her,
20   'Why would you never be afraid of burglars
with your husband in the house?'

She calls a meeting at Eyre Square
for half three that Saturday.
Standing on a chair, wiping her hands
25   on her apron, she explains.

'One day,' she says, in a cross voice,
'The dog disobeyed my husband
and my husband beat him across the head
with a whip made from horse hair.

30   That is why I am not afraid of burglars
with my husband in the house.'

Rita Anne Higgins

The Wife's Story

What with his taking small bets on the footy,
While keeping out a sharp eye for the Bulls,
And what with laying off among other bookies
Who masqueraded as both knaves and fools;

5   What with his ringing up those drunken mates –
The one who sang 'Jack Doolan' in the bar,
The fat one and the one with smelly feet –
And talking to the bloke who tuned his car;

What with his ringing up the spirit merchant
10 And with those calls he made too low to hear
But which, she long suspected, were his urgent
Demands on girls with easy yellow hair;

And what with the invitations he'd refuse,
The telephone was never hers to use.

Chris Wallace-Crabbe

Spider Woman

She spun the argument
with a thread
he could not follow

perfecting
5   the delicate construction

until he
unsuspecting

fell
entangled

10 to
his

gentle destruction.

Shamshad Khan

Women's Liberation

Hello sweetie home from work

I've cooked your dinner

I'm a berk.

Sue May

Thinking and writing

1   Two of these poems (on pages 21–4) are written by men, the other three by women. Are there any noticeable differences in tone between the two sets of writers? Give examples to support your views.

2   What would you say is the balance of negative to positive presentations of women in these poems (based on your understanding of their tone and overall meaning)?

All of these are modern, contemporary poems. Rudyard Kipling's 'The Female of the Species', however, was written in the early part of this century. This is a long poem with some difficult references and language. Read the poem and concentrate on what Kipling says about the female as an animal and a human being.

The Female of the Species

When the Himalayan peasant meets the he-bear in his pride,
He shouts to scare the monster, who will often turn aside,
But the she-bear thus accosted rends the peasant tooth and nail.
For the female of the species is more deadly than the male.

5 When Nag the basking cobra hears the careless foot of man,
He will sometimes wriggle sideways and avoid it if he can.
But his mate makes no such motion where she camps besides the trail.
For the female of the species is more deadly than the male.

When the early Jesuit father preached to Hurons and Choctaws,
10 They prayed to be delivered from the vengeance of the squaws.
'Twas the women, not the warriors, turned those stark enthusiasts pale.
For the female of the species is more deadly than the male.

Man's timid heart is bursting with the things he must not say,
For the Woman that God gave him isn't his to give away;
15 But when hunter meets with husband, each confirms the other's tale –
The female of the species is more deadly than the male.

Man, a bear in most relations – worm and savage otherwise, –
Man propounds negotiations, Man accepts the compromise.
Very rarely will he squarely push the logic of a fact
20 To its ultimate conclusion in unmitigated act.

Fear, or foolishness, impels him, ere he lay the wicked low,
To concede some form of trial even to his fiercest foe.
Mirth obscene diverts his anger – Doubt and Pity oft perplex
Him in dealing with an issue – to the scandal of The Sex!

25 But the Woman that God gave him, every fibre of her frame
Proves her launched for one sole issue, armed and engined for the same;
And to serve that single issue, lest the generations fail,
The female of the species must be deadlier than the male.

She who faces Death by torture for each life beneath her breast
30 May not deal in doubt or pity – must not swerve for fact or jest.
These be purely male diversions – not in these her honour dwells.
She, the Other Law we live by, is that Law and nothing else.

She can bring no more to living than the powers that make her great
As the Mother of the Infant and the Mistress of the Mate.
35   And when Babe and Man are lacking and she strides unclaimed to claim
Her right as femme (and baron), her equipment is the same.

She is wedded to convictions — in default of grosser ties;
Her contentions are her children, Heaven help him who denies! —
He will meet no suave discussion, but the instant, white-hot, wild,
40   Wakened female of the species warring as for spouse and child.

Unprovoked and awful charges — even so the she-bear fights,
Speech that drips, corrodes, and poisons — even so the cobra bites;
Scientific vivisection of one nerve till it is raw
And the victim writhes in anguish — like the Jesuit with the squaw!

45   So it comes that Man, the coward, when he gathers to confer
With his fellow-braves in council, dare not leave a place for her
Where, at war with Life and Conscience, he uplifts his erring hands
To some God of Abstract Justice — which no woman understands.

And Man knows it! Knows, moreover, that the Woman that God gave him
50   Must command but may not govern — shall enthral but not enslave him.
And *She* knows, because She warns him, and Her instincts never fail,
That the Female of Her Species is more deadly than the Male!

Rudyard Kipling

Thinking and discussion

1 List the references to female animals and humans (e.g. 'she-bear' and 'squaw').
Pick out any examples which are definitely positive and definitely negative.

2 In considering both positive and negative tones, in what two opposing ways could
you describe the meaning of Kipling's refrain 'For the female of the species is more
deadly than the male'?

3 This is a very long poem and you may not follow all of the things that Kipling is
saying. But, by dipping in and out of parts of the poem, can you spot any changes in
what is being said about women from the early **stanzas** to the later ones?

Just for fun, you might like to compare Kipling's poem with the song of the same title
by the group Space.

Female of the species

A thousand thundering thrills
await me
Facing insurmountable odds
gratefully
5 The female of the species is more
deadly than the male
Shock Shock Horror Horror
Shock Shock Horror
I'll shout myself hoarse for your
10 supernatural force
The female of the species is more
deadly than the male
Oh she deals in witchcraft
And one kiss and I'm zapped
15 Oh how can heaven hold a place for me
When a girl like you has cast a spell
on me
Oh how can heaven hold a place for me
When a girl like you has cast a spell
20 on me

Frankenstein and Dracula have
nothing on you
Jekyll and Hyde join the back of
the queue
25 The female of the species is more
deadly than the male
Oh she wants to conquer the
world completely
But there she'll conquer
30 me discreetly
The female of the species is more
deadly than the male
Oh she deals in witchcraft
and one kiss and I'm zapped
35 Oh how can heaven hold a place for me
When a girl like you has cast a spell
on me
Oh how can heaven hold a place for me
When a girl like you has cast a spell
40 on me

Space

Thinking and discussion

In the song, women are compared with witchcraft, Dracula, Frankenstein
(his creature, presumably) and Jekyll and Hyde! By looking at all of the **lyrics**, can you
present a case for this NOT giving the song a negative tone?

Wrap it up

You have now read a wide range of poems with varying tones. There are poems like
'Base Details' which present their tone of voice quite clearly, and poems like 'Life
Doesn't Frighten Me At All' which might be more ambivalent. Remember to listen
carefully for clues which will help you to hear the poet's tone and give you a head-
start in your understanding of its meaning and message. A poet with a positive, happy
tone is probably describing happy events! A poet with a negative or satirical tone …
now there's a can of worms! This will lead us on to the next chapter and an
exploration of **metaphors** and other poetic techniques.

Techniques

What is meant by poetic techniques? Techniques are the tools of the trade that a poet uses to write poetry. They are the ways and means used to get a message across. Their purpose is to help the reader, or listener, to see, hear, feel and think more vividly about the subject being described. By creating pictures in the mind's eye, mimicking sounds and other devices, meaning can be conveyed in new and memorable ways.

Techniques
checklist

Creating pictures

The use of poetic techniques can produce unusual and original descriptions that create vivid or even outrageous pictures in your mind. They can also create sensations of the thing being described, like intense heat or cold. These will help you see and feel the subject-matter being described in new, memorable and meaningful ways. Pictures can be created in poems using:

- image
- metaphor
- simile
- personification.

Sound effects

The use of poetic techniques can produce harsh or soothing descriptions which create distinct noises, particularly when read aloud, that help you to hear the movement of an activity or the actual sound of a thing, animal or person being described. This can add considerable realism as well as imaginative qualities to a poem. Sound effects can be produced in poems using:

- alliteration
- assonance
- onomatopoeia.

Layout

The use of poetic techniques can produce structures that place emphasis on words or phrases. This can create surprise and shock in reading the unexpected word or sudden shift of meaning. This is achieved in poems by using:

- enjambement.

Pictures in words
Imagery

Read 'Tractor' by Ted Hughes. For this first reading, enjoy the story-line.

Tractor

The tractor stands frozen – an agony
To think of. All night
Snow packed its open entrails. Now a head-
   pincering gale,
A spill of molten ice, smoking snow,
5 Pours into its steel.
At white heat of numbness it stands
In the aimed hosing of ground-level fieriness.

It defies flesh and won't start.
Hands are like wounds already
10 Inside armour gloves, and feet are unbelievable
As if the toe-nails were all just torn off.
I stare at it in hatred. Beyond it
The copse hisses – capitulates miserably
In the fleeing, failing light. Starlings,
15 A dirtier sleetier snow, blow smokily,
   unendingly, over
Towards plantations Eastward.
All the time the tractor is sinking
Through the degrees, deepening
Into its hell of ice.
20 The starting lever
Cracks its action, like a snapping knuckle.
The battery is alive – but like a lamb
Trying to nudge its solid-frozen mother –
While the seat claims my buttock-bones, bites
25 With the space-cold of earth, which it has joined
In one solid lump.

I squirt commercial sure-fire
Down the black throat – it just coughs.
It ridicules me – a trap of iron stupidity
30 I've stepped into. I drive the battery
As if I were hammering and hammering

The frozen arrangement to pieces with
   a hammer
And it jabbers laughing pain-crying mockingly
Into happy life.

35 And stands
Shuddering itself full of heat, seeming to
   enlarge slowly
Like a demon demonstrating
A more-than-usually-complete materialization –
Suddenly it jerks from its solidarity
40 With the concrete, and lurches towards
   a stanchion
Bursting with superhuman well-being
   and abandon
Shouting Where Where?

Worse iron is waiting. Power-lift kneels,
Levers awake imprisoned deadweight,
45 Shackle-pins bedded in cast-iron cow-shit.
The blind and vibrating condemned obedience
Of iron to the cruelty of iron,
Wheels screeched out of their night-locks –

Fingers
50 Among the tormented
Tonnage and burning of iron

Eyes
Weeping in the wind of chloroform

And the tractor, streaming with sweat,
55 Raging and trembling and rejoicing.

Ted Hughes

Read 'Tractor' again and, this time, concentrate on the descriptions and the pictures Hughes evokes. Think about how these are being used to make you experience the same intense cold. Consider the ways in which they are being used to appeal to your senses.

Thinking and writing

1   Using the headings 'Sight', 'Sound' and 'Touch', find examples to demonstrate how these senses are being referred to in 'Tractor', e.g.

Sight	Sound	Touch
'A spill of molten ice, smoking snow, Pours into its steel'	'The starting lever Cracks its action, like a snapping knuckle'	'and feet are unbelievable As if the toe-nails were all just torn off'

2   This poem tells a detailed story. Using 50 words (or as near to this as you can) retell the story by presenting only the main and essential details.

3   Write a sentence to explain what has been 'lost' by telling your shortened, factual account.

4   If I were writing about the imagery in 'Tractor', I would focus on two **images** in particular. The first describes the severity of the cold: 'and feet are unbelievable/ As if the toe-nails were all just torn off'. This suggests a painful sense impression and associates torn flesh with ice and snow! The second image helps me to see just how frozen everything has become: 'Levers awake imprisoned deadweight,/Shackle-pins bedded in cast-iron cow-shit'. Pick out two of *your* favourite images and explain how they work.

5   The poem works towards a crescendo. If you don't already know, find out what 'crescendo' means and write a sentence explaining how Hughes' poem achieves this.

6   What are Hughes' feelings about his tractor by the end of the poem? Use three lines from the poem to justify your explanation.

Simile

While images, pictures and sense impressions may be evoked by poetic description, a **simile** is a particular image created by comparing two distinctly different things. This tends to link the shared qualities of both things. Similes can be identified by use of the words 'like' or 'as'.

Thinking and discussion

Pick out two similes in Ted Hughes' 'Tractor' and explain their purpose within the poem.

'The Waitress and the Nights of the Round Table' by Lemn Sissay is a longer poem and you should read it carefully twice before moving on to the following writing and discussion tasks.

the Waitress and the Nights of the Round Table

Each immaculate table a near perfect reflection of the next,
A 40s Hollywood formation dance captured in time
In black and white.
On the mahogany, polished as a morning pond,
5   Each table-cloth flapped as swans' wings
And each landing perfect.
She made pieces of butter intricate
As the hand-woven curls in a judge's wig
And if not so legal and final
10   They'd be a crest of waves
Caught in yellow sunshine.

Each serviette a silent smiling signet born in her hands,
Each flower arranged as if grown for this evening
Sucks water slowly through the stem and raises its neck.
15   They bathe in the light flitting from cut crystal vase
And stand assertive in centre tables, waiting.
She picks a speck of dust from a spotless unspeckled carpet,
Her reflection buckles in the neck of a mercurial fork
While the solemn red candles wait too,
20   To weep their red tears.

She pauses as a mother would for a moment
In the front room, before the visitors arrive,
In admiration and slight concern
And bathes in the symmetry and silence
25   And the oddness of order—
Even the tables seemed to brace themselves as she left.

The picture was distorted when she returned from the kitchens.
A hungry hoard of steak-sawing, wine-guzzling,
Spirit-sapping, double-breasted suits had grabbed their places.
30 They dug their spiked elbows into the wilting backs of tables.
The table-cloth dripped congealed red wine from its quiet hanging corners
And the sounds of their grunts, growls, their slurping,
Their gulping and tearing crept in and invaded the hall.
But a black swan amongst a sea of serrated cutlery, she soared just above
35 And wove a delicate determined ballet in between and invisible.
She walked for miles that evening, balancing platters,
Pinafore-perfect hair clipped so not to slip.
The wine warmed and the candles cried.

In the background of the laughter of their greed—
40 The guttural sound of wolves.
She retrieved a carcass of lamb, poured red,
And didn't notice the bloodshot eyes slide over her
Nor the claws stretching and puncturing leather brogues,
Scratching the wooden floor, nor their irritation at her.
45 One mauled a mobile phone with a clumsy paw.
The alcohol-fueled change was taking hold
And together they could be and become who they really were.
Wolves. Wolves in their pride. Wolves in their pack.
Their lower jaws had stretched and eyes slitted—
50 Some even bayed as wolves, heads flicking side to side,
Tongues slipping low, slow and deliberately from their mouths
And curling sensually to their snouts. The wolf has a permanent smile.
It grew, first half-cough, half-bark. One paw banged on the table,
Another banged and another and another and another
55 Until the whole hall echoed with the unified clatter
Of the guttural phlegm-flicked word that brought them together.
'Gerni gerni gerni gerni,' they chanted. 'Ggerni ggerni ggerni,' they
    chanted faster
'Ggerni ggerni ggerni ggerni,' faster and faster and faster and faster
'Ggerniggerniggernigggerniggerniggerni.'
60 She turned to her colleagues who stood by the kitchen entrance,
But their eyes! Their eyes slipped sideways away from her.
They too were wolves! Her lips parted for her voice and the room
    hushed itself
But for the slipping of saliva from their jaws and the flickering candles
And the dripping of the red wine from the table-cloth.
65 As instructed by her manager, she, smiling politely,
Asked a wolf, 'More coffee sir?'

Lemn Sissay

Thinking and writing

1 Pick out and comment on two or three similes (comparisons using the words *like* or *as*) used in the opening two stanzas of Sissay's poem to give the reader visual images of the waitress's perfection at her job. Describe how these are used to convey her skill and dedication.

2 Describe at what point in the poem the tone changes. How does Sissay establish this changed atmosphere?

3 In the first half of the poem, various similes are used to compare the waitress and her activities. In the second half of the poem an extended metaphor (when one thing 'becomes' another) is used to characterise the customers eating at the table as wolves. The final long stanza reveals the most powerful and disturbing aspects of the poem's 'story'. In what ways does Sissay add more literal detail to support his metaphoric descriptions?

4 This poem was commissioned for a Radio Four programme about a trial involving a waitress who had been racially abused at a dinner party. Write a paragraph on the ways in which you feel Sissay has presented both the woman's dignity and suffering in this incident. In what ways have you as a reader been made to understand and sympathise with her experience?

Metaphor

While a simile creates images by comparing different things, a metaphor is more sophisticated. It actually transforms one thing into another. By working through the following poems you should begin to appreciate the significance and power of metaphor. A good poem to begin our exploration with is Sylvia Plath's, 'Metaphors'.

Metaphors

I'm a riddle in nine syllables,
An elephant, a ponderous house,
A melon strolling on two tendrils.
O red fruit, ivory, fine timbers!
5   This loaf's big with its yeasty rising.
Money's new-minted in this fat purse.
I'm a means, a stage, a cow in calf.
I've eaten a bag of green apples,
Boarded the train there's no getting off.

Sylvia Plath

Discussion and writing

1 Discuss with a partner what you think 'Metaphors' is actually describing. Consider the opening line carefully and then count the number of lines in the poem. You should also count the number of **syllables** in each line.

2 Why has the poet used these various metaphors to describe the same thing? How do the different metaphors help you to *see, feel* and *think* about a pregnancy in different ways?

3 Write a sentence describing how 'A melon strolling on two tendrils' helps you to *see* the speaker.

4 Write a sentence on how 'I'm a means, a stage, a cow in calf' gets you to *feel* what it's like being pregnant. Then explain how this gets you to *think* about her attitude to pregnancy (which is a clue to the overall tone of the poem).

5 Produce your own definition of a metaphor. (*See* the Glossary for another definition.)

The next poem is also written as a set of riddles for you to solve. The riddles are descriptions of familiar things on Earth viewed through the eyes of a visiting Martian. Most of these riddles are, in fact, metaphors.

A Martian Sends a
Postcard Home

Caxtons are mechanical birds with many wings
and some are treasured for their markings —

they cause the eyes to melt
or the body to shriek without pain.

5 I have never seen one fly, but
sometimes they perch on the hand.

Mist is when the sky is tired of flight
and rests its soft machine on ground:

then the world is dim and bookish
10 like engravings under tissue paper.

Rain is when the earth is television.
It has the property of making colours darker.

Model T is a room with the lock inside —
a key is turned to free the world

15 for movement, so quick there is a film
to watch for anything missed.

But time is tied to the wrist
or kept in a box, ticking with impatience.

In homes, a haunted apparatus sleeps,
20 that snores when you pick it up.

If the ghost cries, they carry it
to their lips and soothe it to sleep

with sounds. And yet, they wake it up
deliberately, by tickling with a finger.

25 Only the young are allowed to suffer
openly. Adults go to a punishment room

with water but nothing to eat.
They lock the door and suffer the noises

alone. No one is exempt
30 and everyone's pain has a different smell.

At night, when all the colours die,
they hide in pairs

and read about themselves —
in colour, with their eyelids shut.

Craig Raine

Writing

There are nine riddles to solve in Raine's poem. As you find each item, write down one Martian phrase that describes it. 'Mist' and 'rain' are obvious clues! Can you find the telephone and video camera? There are five more (lines 31–4 describe two things).

Follow John Citizen's use of an extended metaphor in his poem 'The Library of Love'.

the Library of Love

I was out of date and antiquarian,
you dusted me off, you're the librarian.
My pages were loose, I was unwinding.
You stapled me together, you're my binding.
5   Frightened to wear my heart
on my sleeve blurb,
too many nouns, you were the verb.
The end of my lines were well overdue,
you paid all my fines, you can renew.
10 I wanted to be a loan,
you took me out.
I was at a loss leader,
you're my proof reader.
When no one credited me, you edited me.
15 And when critics rubbished me,
you published me.
From the shelves below to the shelves above,
you're the librarian in the library of love.

John Citizen

Writing

One of the best ways to appreciate the use of poetic techniques is to try using them yourself! It isn't as easy as it looks, but with a little effort and imagination you can certainly have a go. Try writing a similar poem to John Citizen's, using one of the following titles (or make up your own):

'The Butchers of Love'
e.g. Forgotten, frozen and uncooked,
you thawed me out and I was hooked …

'The Garage of Love'
e.g. My engine groaned but wouldn't start,
you put new sparkplugs into my heart …

(OK – you don't have to be as soppy as the second one!)

The poem 'Valentine' by Carol Ann Duffy uses metaphors and other techniques to describe love in an original and powerful way.

Valentine

Not a red rose or a satin heart.

I give you an onion.
It is a moon wrapped in brown paper.
It promises light
5   like the careful undressing of love.

Here.
It will blind you with tears
like a lover.
It will make your reflection
10 a wobbling photo of grief.

I am trying to be truthful.

Not a cute card or a kissogram.

I give you an onion.
Its fierce kiss will stay on your lips,
15 possessive and faithful
as we are,
for as long as we are.

Take it.
Its platinum loops shrink to a wedding-ring,
20 if you like.
Lethal.
Its scent will cling to your fingers,
cling to your knife.

Carol Ann Duffy

When beginning to work out the meaning of a poem you should always start with the title. This one gives us an excellent, early clue! There is something very different about this valentine and Duffy tells us that she will send an onion as hers. Are we meant to believe this? If she isn't a deranged cook, we might presume that we shouldn't take it literally! As increasingly sophisticated readers of poetry, we can deduce that this is going to be the poem's central metaphor.

Thinking and writing

1 Look closely at lines 2–5 of 'Valentine'. As well as referring to the onion, there are two other metaphors used. Write them down and explain their purpose within the poem, that is, how they get us to see what is being described.

2 Look closely at lines 6–10. How is a particular effect caused by an onion linked to another effect caused by being in love? At this point in the poem, what would you say is its tone and therefore the writer's feelings about love?

3 Look closely at lines 13–17. In what way are we meant to feel about the onion now (consider which of our senses is being appealed to)? Is the tone in this stanza negative or positive? Is it the same as in lines 6–10? If not, what does a changing tone tell us about the nature of love?

4 The final stanza returns to a visual image. If the mention of a 'wedding-ring' produces a romantic image, explain why you think Duffy calls this 'Lethal'. Write a few sentences on how you think this dramatic ending gets you to think about the poet's attitude to and presentation of love.

Carol Ann Duffy uses her extended metaphor of an onion to generate serious and powerful ideas about the way that we celebrate love. A traditional gift is called into question with imagination and realism. By offering an onion instead of a valentine card as a declaration of love, these two unlike objects become linked and draw extra meaning from each other. The force of the metaphor compels the reader to consider the subject matter in interesting and unusual ways.

Personification

Related to metaphor is the poetic device of **personification**. This is where an inanimate object or abstract concept is given life or human qualities.

Thinking and writing

1 Write down an example of personification in Craig Raine's 'A Martian Sends a Postcard Home'.

2 Looking back to Ted Hughes' poem, 'Tractor', you will see that he personifies the tractor, or gives it human characteristics. Explore the effect this has and how it enhances the meaning of the poem.

Sound effects

The sounds made by the words and **rhythms** of a poem also help the reader hear or visualise what is being described. These sounds may be as realistic as possible to mimic the thing, activity or sound being presented, or they may be exaggerated to make a particular point.

Onomatopoeia, alliteration and assonance

Edward Kamau Brathwaite's poem 'Ogun' is full of sounds which imitate his uncle's woodworking shop. Along with the minute observation of detail, this creates a sense of being present in the workshop while his uncle works.

My uncle made chairs, tables, balanced doors on, dug out
coffins, smoothing the white wood out

with plane and quick sandpaper until
it shone like his short-sighted glasses.

5 The knuckles of his hands were sil-
vered knobs of nails hit, hurt and flat-

tened out with blast of heavy hammer. He was knock-knee'd, flat-
footed and his clip clop sandals slapped across the concrete

flooring of his little shop where canefield mulemen and a fleet
10 of Bedford lorry drivers dropped in to scratch themselves and talk.

There was no shock of wood, no beam
of light mahogany his saw teeth couldn't handle.

When shaping squares for locks, a key hole
care tapped rat tat tat upon the handle

15 of his humpbacked chisel. Cold
world of wood caught fire as he whittled: rectangle

window frames, the intersecting x of fold-
ing chairs, triangle

trellises, the donkey
20 box-cart in its squeaking square.

But he was poor and most days he was hungry.
Imported cabinets with mirrors, formica table

tops, spine-curving chairs made up of tubes, with hollow
steel-like bird bones that sat on rubber ploughs,

25   thin beds, stretched not on boards, but blue high-tensioned cables,
were what the world preferred.

And yet he had a block of wood that would have baffled them.
With knife and gimlet care he worked away at this on Sundays,

explored its knotted hurts, cutting his way
30   along its yellow whorls until his hands could feel

how it had swelled and shivered, breathing air,
its weathered green burning to rings of time,

its contoured grain still tuned to roots and water.
And as he cut, he heard the creak of forests:

35   green lizard faces gulped, grey memories with moth
eyes watched him from their shadows, soft

liquid tendrils leaked among the flowers
and a black rigid thunder he had never heard within his hammer

came stomping up the trunks. And as he worked within his shattered
40   Sunday shop, the wood took shape: dry shuttered

eyes, slack anciently everted lips, flat
ruined face, eaten by pox, ravaged by rat

and woodworm, dry cistern mouth, cracked
gullet crying for the desert, the heavy black

45   enduring jaw; lost pain, lost iron;
emerging woodwork image of his anger.

Edward Kamau Brathwaite

In 'Ogun' the techniques of **sound patterns** are used to help create the overall meaning. The mimicking of sounds is known as **onomatopoeia**. **Alliteration** is a pattern built up by repeating consonants. **Assonance** is a patterning of repeating vowel sounds. All of these poetic techniques can be considered as 'sound effects', like those in a movie to help make the pictures and action realistic.

Thinking and writing

1 In 'Ogun', was the work done in the shop hard or easy? To answer this question fully you could refer to the sounds associated with the descriptions. For example, the uncle's knuckles are hardened by the rough work. We know this because they are described as 'sil-/vered knobs of nails' that have been 'hit, hurt and flat-/tened'. In addition to this direct description, we have the hard, consonantal sounds of the letters k, n, b and t. The words are short and clipped like the short, sharp hammer blows hitting the fingers. Also, the short vowels in 'hit', 'hurt' and 'flat' sound like breath being expelled with the physical effort of the work. Two words are split – perhaps to convey being hit, like being knocked from one line into the next.

2 Look at line 8 'footed and his clip clop sandals slapped across the concrete'. Alliteration and onomatopoeia are used here together to help create a particular sound. Referring to the Glossary as necessary, write down other examples of these techniques.

3 Look at lines 2–4. Here we have 's-' and 'sh-' sounds to imitate sanding and planing. Are these hard or soft sounds? Find two examples each of hard and soft sound patterns (which may or may not use alliteration and onomatopoeia) in the rest of the poem. Write these out and explain what they are trying to describe.

4 Go back and look at lines 20–26 in 'Tractor'. Write down one example of onomatopoeia used to convey the sound of the tractor trying to start.

5 Write down one example of alliteration used to describe the harsh and hard feeling of the cold.

All of the techniques we have looked at so far (and more) are used in Roger Robinson's poem about clubbing. In 'The Last Dance' he has a serious message about how dancing makes him forget the 'stress', 'towerblocks' and 'dole-queue blues' of his life. He needs to convey how the music can gradually help him to rise above this. By using sound patterns, layout, metaphor, rhyme and rhythm (*see* Chapter 3 Types), this poem, like 'Tractor', works towards a crescendo.

The Last Dance

I step in the party and vibrate
from late night bassline therapy.
Left my stress at the coat room
I've come to dance a wounded mind
5 before it bleeds insanity lead me to a dancefloor
to nod thoughts to the tempo.
Satin skinned sisters
boogie curves to a beat,
as brothers seek solace
10 in sexy sillhouettes
of hearts flowering in dark corners.
But back to my beat
Stylus sliding lyrics for my mind set,
grooves soothe the rest.
15 Ears suck soul notes for energy
Hi hats shift my hipbones
break beats shake my waistline
hearts and bass beats synchronize
and for four minute moments,
20 I am music
yeah,
I'm the ghetto lullaby
floating from towerblocks
caressing young faded heads
25 on the corner.
I'm the embraceable tune
of first time lovers
thumping funky rhythms
on a rickety bed.
30 Yeah, I am music
so I dance.
I dance steps
delicate as barefeet
on a broken glass mile.

35 Drowning in music
catching smiles and breaths on melody.
Dole queue blues drench my T-shirt
my dirty nikes stepping rhythm
from a month of tears.
40 DJ picks up the pace
and the place jumps and waves
hands swaying in the air
a testifying chorus of pain.
DJ flinging down commandments plastic.
45 Then music's spirit leaps
out the speakers
on a tidal bass
breaking on our faces.
Baptised reborn refreshed
50 I dance
I dance tears of sour sweet sweat
in slowly choreographed steps of death,
and the only thought I can hold is this tune
and if this party ends it's too soon
55 so I dance, I dance
in clubs of dark damp grief
as hips of hurt sway some relief
I scream
I jump
60 I smoke
I drink
I groove
I dance
I dance
65 like this dance may be our last.

Roger Robinson

Thinking and writing

1 Pick out and comment on some of the techniques used in 'The Last Dance' to create a sense of being at the party or club and hearing the dancing. For each technique, remember to explain how it helps the poet's purpose.

2 Notice how the last stanza introduces rhyme into the poem. Why do you think Robinson does this at this point?

Compare Robinson's poem with 'September Assignment' by Mike Kivi. Both use a party, club or rave as their setting (although Kivi uses other settings as well). Both use particular techniques to recreate the sound and movement of partying and dancing.

September Assignment

Write about 500 words on one of the following:
i)   My summer holiday
ii) Adolescent relationships
iii) Pop music

Deep in the heat of a camp site rave,
Little Tina Turnbull dances the night,
Filled with the thrill of a chemical wave,
Flying in the flash of fluorescent light.
5 Driven by the rhythm of a high speed laser,
Pulse pumped hard with a pocket full of pills,
High as a kite, sharp as a razor,
Stuttering steps in the strobe light stills.
Boogying close as the beat drives harder,
10 Hippity together to the disco door,
Sinking in the seat of a clapped out Lada,
Scrabbling for the condoms on the cold car floor.
Back to the caravan at half past three
(Parents paralytic on the double divan)
15 Worried over syphilis and HIV,
Pimples that appeared instead of a tan.
Packed next morning sitting in the car,
Eyes shut tight with her walkman on,
Dreams of a foetus in a marmalade jar,
20 Childhood, babies, holidays gone.
Rainclouds form on the fading hill,
Wipers start to squeak on the fly-stained screen,
Eyes turned cold in the wintry chill
As the radio plays sweet little sixteen.

Mike Kivi

Thinking and writing

1 Look closely at lines 4–8 of Kivi's poem. How are the language and techniques used here similar to 'The Last Dance'?

2 What is the tone of 'September Assignment'? Is this the same as 'The Last Dance'? Refer to specific words and images to support your comments.

3 What is **ironic** (*see* Glossary) about the last line of 'September Assignment'?

Before we leave this focus of sound effects altogether, here's one more example of onomatopoeia. It's in John Hegley's poem 'A Fisher of Words'.

A fisher of words

legs dangle
    at an angle
        on the slow-wetted harbourside
          where I netted the tide
5   well
      just a tiny trickle
    of the plop glop slack slop
  slip back slap
and tickle

John Hegley

Layout
Enjambement

The last specific technique we will look at is the use of **enjambement**. This is where the sense of completion at the end of a line is not achieved and the words 'run on' into the next line. This technique is usually used to focus attention on the word or phrase in the following line. It can shock when a particular word is placed at the beginning of the following line, or surprise when the meaning is unexpected. Look at a comic example in the last two lines of another John Hegley poem, 'The Firework'.

The Firework

up in the sky go the rockets
little Albert gets a big surprise
and his big round eyes
light up in their sockets
5   the rockets
came out of his trouser pockets

John Hegley

'The Firework' demonstrates the comic effect of surprise or shock in the following line. Here's another example, this time from the American poet, Gerald Locklin, and his poem 'what i learned from watching the pink panther cartoon festival'.

what i learned from watching the pink panther cartoon festival

never position yourself behind a door,
beneath the matterhorn,
downstream from a dam,
in the middle of an intersection,
5   or under a truck.

and for god's sake
never never never never never
deposit a bomb in

what you are sure is
10 someone else's pocket.

Gerald Locklin

Rather than look at examples within whole poems, it would be useful to look at a few individual lines taken from a range of poems. A memorable line using enjambement for a specific effect comes from Wilfred Owen's poem 'The Send-off'. In this poem Owen describes men at a train station who are being sent off to fight in the First World War. Wives and girlfriends have come to say their goodbyes, and some have pinned flower sprays on the soldiers' tunics:

> 'Their breasts were stuck all white with wreath and spray
> As men's are, dead.'

You can see immediately how there is a shock effect in the following line. This compares these men and their fresh flowers with men who are dead and have floral wreaths as symbols of death.

The use of enjambement here is complemented by making the first line an **iambic pentameter** (*see* Glossary) and the second only four syllables long. The effect of moving abruptly from one long flowing line to a short and sharp line adds to the shock.

In Seamus Heaney's poem 'The Early Purges', the first two stanzas reveal the continued use of enjambement for particular effects.

The Early Purges

> I was six when I first saw kittens drown.
> Dan Taggart pitched them, "the scraggy wee shits",
> Into a bucket; a frail metal sound,
>
> Soft paws scraping like mad. But their tiny din
> 5 Was soon soused. They were slung on the snout
> Of the pump and the water pumped in.
>
> *Seamus Heaney*

Look closely at lines 3 and 4. First, there is the shock that the kittens are thrown 'Into a bucket' and secondly the sudden image of their 'Soft paws scraping like mad'.

Reminder

All of the techniques we have explored either create images or make you see, hear and feel the things that are being described. As well as being able to identify the techniques, whenever you refer to them in your writing, you must also be able to explain their *purpose and effect* to gain the highest marks. At GCSE, the three important steps to take when writing about this and other aspects of poetry are:

1 Identification – being able to describe the technique/feature

2 Examination – being able to explain its particular purpose and effect

3 Exploration – being able to comment on its development in the poem and how the writer is being original or dynamic; relating this to other poems/poets.

To help you remember these points, the following 'Mantra' could be learned by heart and recited in your head before answering poetry exam questions or completing poetry coursework assignments.

I will not mention the word **metaphor**

unless I can say what it is being used for[1]

I will not mention the word **simile**

unless I can say what *like* and *as* are meant to achieve

I will not mention the word **personification**

unless I can say what *giving life* should do to my imagination

I will not mention the word **alliteration**

unless I can say how the sounds add a sudden sensation

I will not mention the word **onomatopoeia**

unless I can make it wheeze and whoosh like a concertina

I will not mention the word

enjambement

unless I can say what the word (or phrase) was moved for[1,2]

[1] Poetic licence: ending a sentence in a preposition!
[2] Assuming we are nearly French in pronunciation!

Comparing techniques

The next two poems, 'To Autumn' by John Keats and 'Blackberrying' by Sylvia Plath, are long and require careful reading. They are good examples of poems employing all of the techniques we have already looked at. After reading them, there is an activity to complete which will draw together your knowledge and understanding of the work done on poetic techniques.

to AUTUMN

Season of mists and mellow fruitfulness,
Close bosom-friend of the maturing sun;
Conspiring with him how to load
    and bless
With fruit the vines that round the
    thatch-eaves run;
5 To bend with apples the moss'd
    cottage-trees,
And fill all fruit with ripeness to the core;
To swell the gourd, and plump the
    hazel shells
With a sweet kernel; to set budding more,
And still more, later flowers for the bees,
10 Until they think warm days will
    never cease,
For Summer has o'erbrimm'd their
    clammy cells.

Who hath not seen thee oft amid
    thy store?
Sometimes whoever seeks abroad
    may find
Thee sitting careless on a granary floor,
15 Thy hair soft-lifted by the winnowing
    wind;
Or on a half-reap'd furrow sound asleep,
Drows'd with the fume of poppies, while
    thy hook
Spares the next swath and all its
    twinèd flowers;
And sometimes like a gleaner thou
    dost keep

20 Steady thy laden head across a brook;
Or by a cider-press, with patient look,
Thou watchest the last oozings, hours
    by hours.

Where are the songs of Spring? Aye,
    where are they?
Think not of them, – thou hast thy
    music too,
25 While barrèd clouds bloom the soft-
    dying day,
And touch the stubble-plains with
    rosy hue;
Then in a wailful choir the small
    gnats mourn
Among the river sallows, borne aloft
Or sinking as the light wind lives or dies;
30 And full-grown lambs loud bleat from
    hilly bourn;
Hedge-crickets sing, and now with
    treble soft
The redbreast whistles from a
    garden-croft;
And gathering swallows
    twitter in the skies.

John Keats

Blackberrying

Nobody in the lane, and nothing, nothing but
  blackberries,
Blackberries on either side, though on the
  right mainly,
A blackberry alley, going down in hooks, and
  a sea
Somewhere at the end of it, heaving. Blackberries
5 Big as the ball of my thumb, and dumb as eyes
Ebon in the hedges, fat
With blue-red juices. These they squander on
  my fingers.
I had not asked for such a blood sisterhood;
  they must love me.
They accommodate themselves to my milk-
  bottle, flattening their sides.

10 Overhead go the choughs in black,
  cacophonous flocks –
Bits of burnt paper wheeling in a blown sky.
Theirs is the only voice, protesting, protesting.
I do not think the sea will appear at all.
The high, green meadows are glowing, as if lit
  from within.
15 I come to one bush of berries so ripe it is a
  bush of flies,

Hanging their bluegreen bellies and their wing
  panes in a Chinese screen.
The honey-feast of the berries has stunned them;
  they believe in heaven.
One more hook and the berries and bushes end.

The only thing to come now is the sea.
20 From between two hills a sudden wind funnels
  at me,
Slapping its phantom laundry in my face.
These hills are too green and sweet to have
  tasted salt.
I follow the sheep path between them. A last
  hook brings me
To the hills' northern face, and the face is
  orange rock
25 That looks out on nothing, nothing but a
  great space
Of white and pewter lights, and a din like
  silversmiths
Beating and beating at an intractable metal.

Sylvia Plath

Writing

By focusing on the poetic techniques used in 'To Autumn' and 'Blackberrying', identify where they are being used and then comment on their purpose and effect (remember the 'Mantra'!).

Look at the following helpful hints. You should make notes in response to these thinking and discussion points to help with the main writing task.

Thinking and discussion

1 How is autumn personified in the opening stanza of Keats' 'To Autumn'? Is this a negative or positive image (look for words to do with increasing things)?

2 What use does Keats make of 'sound' techniques? (Look particularly in the last stanza.)

3 Look at lines 5–7 in Plath's 'Blackberrying'. On what is the line structure focusing your attention?

4 What is the meaning of 'blood-sisterhood'?

5 Look at lines 10–11. How is the image achieved? What other images are created in this stanza?

6 Look at line 21. There are two definite techniques used here. What are their purpose and effect?

7 The last two lines make you see and feel what is being described. How does this happen?

8 Write about which of these two poems you prefer and why, referring in particular to how each poem makes you see, hear, feel and think about the subject-matter. Remember that they were written at different times: 'To Autumn' is a pre-1900 poem; 'Blackberrying' is contemporary (modern). Does this affect your choice?

Wrap it up

You have now looked at a wide range of poetic techniques (or devices) and seen how they can produce powerful images and sounds in the writing of poetry. In Hughes' poem 'Tractor', he appeals to the reader's senses to create vivid pictures of a frozen tractor and surroundings, stuttering sounds of a stubborn engine, and numbing sensations of winter cold. These bring alive for the reader the experience being described. In poems like 'September Assignment', the imagery and sounds add realism as well as clues to tone and message through their negative and harsh suggestions. Remember that most poetry is metaphorical and that related techniques are used to describe situations and experiences in unusual and engaging ways for the reader. Sometimes an experience cannot be explained in a literal way. Remember that when you are writing about these techniques, you must comment on the purpose and effect they have.

Types

There are many types of poem. When reading and studying a poem, you will need to determine what type it is. This means considering its structure and layout on the page; and also its form, for example whether it is a sonnet or free verse. All of these elements may contribute to the poem's overall meaning. Therefore a poet might choose a particular structure (or lack of one), to underpin the message of the poem.

How is the poem organised? Some poems are organised into groups of lines called stanzas (*see* Glossary); some are not. The **quatrain** (*see* Glossary) is a popular four-line stanza. Within a poem, the stanzas often share a **rhyme scheme** but in some poems the stanzas do not rhyme. There might be a particular rhythm throughout the poem or just the occasional rhythmic line. Some poems are very precisely organised and others seem quite random. Some modern poems appear on the page in eccentric shapes. All of these possibilities should be considered when reading and studying a poem.

Types checklist

Rhyme	The use of rhyme can date poetry or indicate a writer's desire to control and shape a poem with particular sounds. Rhyme schemes might be playful and they can be an integral part of a traditional form of poetry. Rhyme can occur:

- at the ends of lines
- within lines
- within stanzas
- in blank verse
- in rhyming couplets
- as perfect rhyme
- as para-rhyme.

Rhythm	The use of rhythm can create beat and movement in a poem as in a dance.

- This might exist because the poem is written to be read aloud – *performance poetry*.
- It could exist to *direct* your eyes and ears to particular words and phrases.

Form

Poems do not have to follow set patterns but, when they do, this might create a particular challenge and discipline for the writer. A poet may choose a traditional form to follow or mock a convention, for example writing a love poem as a sonnet. The shape and structure of a poem can be as important as the words within it. Poems may take the following forms:

- epic
- ballad
- ode
- lyric poem
- narrative poem
- haiku
- sonnet
- free verse.

Rhyme
The power of rhyme

I realised the power of rhyme within my first hour on the infant school playground. "Do you like jelly?" I was asked. "No," I replied … "I'll punch you in the belly!" I was playfully advised. Do you like blancmange! I'll tread on your foot – so much less effective.

John Hegley

We'll start by looking at two examples of bad rhyming in poems! This is a good place to start because so many students think that poems must rhyme. If you read a range of poems, however, you will soon discover that this is not the case. The two poems are 'Poem in Blank Rhyme' (from *Short Lyrics*) by Glyn Maxwell, and a poem written by William McGonagall praising a Reverend George Gilfillan.

Poem in Blank Rhyme

This isn't very difficult to do.
The sky's pink, the morning pretty new.

Last night I met a mate from the old crew.
We walked too far too late and turned a U

5   Out of the woods as it got dark. He knew
I'd spend the evening talking about you

But didn't mind and, when we had to queue,
He made the time fly quickly with his two

Dozen unfunny jokes, plus a big clue
10   About his own big heart. Well the sky's blue

Now over there, I'm standing in the dew,
Remembering and hoping. But it's true:

Days are very many. Days are few.
I want to be with someone and you're who.

Glynn Maxwell

Thinking and writing

1   The title of Maxwell's poem refers to blank rhyme. There is a term called **blank verse** which refers to unrhymed lines of iambic pentameter, a verse form closest to the natural rhythms of English speech. What could Maxwell be referring to (think about the general meaning of the word 'blank')?

2   How do the first and last lines of his poem give us clues to use (a rhyme!) in working out whether he is serious in his choice of rhymes?

3   All of the rhyming words contain one syllable. Does this have any significance?

4   Assuming that you are working out how simple and rather uninspiring these rhymes are, consider whether you think this is therefore a poorly written poem without any particular meaning. Give reasons for your answer.

5   The poem seems to describe a person thinking about someone liked or loved. It ends with the simple, if ungrammatical line, 'I want to be with someone and you're who'. Write a sentence to explain how this simple statement, and the simple rhyme, might actually give the poem a meaning we haven't yet considered.

This is a difficult poem because it is not clear what is being said, and the way in which it is written, with the often silly rhymes, is too obvious to ignore. This could, however, be part of its charm!

Rev. George Gilfillan of Dundee

'Rev. George Gilfillan of Dundee,
There is none can you excel;
You have boldly rejected the Confession of Faith.
And defended your cause right well.

5 'The first time I heard him speak
'Twas in the Kinnaird Hall,
Lecturing on the Garibaldi movement,
As loud as he could bawl.

'He is a liberal gentleman
10 To the poor while in distress,
And for his kindness unto them
The Lord will surely bless.

'My blessing on his noble form.
And on his lofty head,
15 May all good angels guard him while living,
And hereafter when he's dead.'

William McGonagall

Consider the following questions to see whether the use of rhyme contributes to McGonagall's poem.

Thinking and writing

1 Make a note of any forced rhymes in this poem (ones that seem to be sledgehammered into rhyming).

2 Comment on how genuine you think the poem's message is. Does the rhyming add to or detract from this?

Rhyming couplets

Shakespeare used rhyme for particular effects in his plays. Long blank verse speeches would often end in strong rhyming **couplets**. This could signal the end to a scene or the conclusion to an argument or important point. In the play, *Macbeth*, Macbeth is about to go and kill the sleeping king Duncan when he hears the sound of a bell being rung. He says:

'Hear it not Duncan, for it is a knell
That summons thee to heaven or to hell'

This perfect rhyme gives a chilling certainty to what he is about to do. Poets will often use rhyme to achieve similar, important and obvious effects. Who better to turn to for an example than William Shakespeare himself and his Sonnet 17 which is actually about writing poetry!

Sonnet 17

Who will believe my verse in time to come,
If it were fill'd with your most high deserts?
Though yet, heaven knows, it is but as a tomb
Which hides your life and shows not half your parts.
5   If I could write the beauty of your eyes
And in fresh numbers number all your graces,
The age to come would say 'This poet lies;
Such heavenly touches ne'er touched earthly faces'.
So should my papers, yellowed with their age,
10   Be scorn'd, like old men of less truth than tongue;
And your true rights be term'd a poet's rage,
And stretched metre of an antique song.
But were some child of yours alive that time,
You should live twice – in it, and in my rhyme.

William Shakespeare

Thinking and writing

1   In Shakespeare's Sonnet 17, why do you think the concluding rhyming couplet (lines 13–14) begins with the word 'But'?

2   Summarise the argument contained in the couplet and explain how the rhyme reinforces this. Does the final couplet answer the thoughts of the preceding 12 lines?

Perfect rhyme

Let's explore other uses of rhyme in two poems by the First World War poet, Wilfred Owen. The first, 'Dulce et Decorum est', is probably the poem he is most famous for.

Dulce et Decorum est

Bent double, like old beggars under sacks,
Knock-kneed, coughing like hags, we cursed through sludge,
Till on the haunting flares we turned our backs,
And towards our distant rest began to trudge.
5 Men marched asleep. Many had lost their boots,
But limped on, blood-shod. All went lame, all blind;
Drunk with fatigue; deaf even to the hoots
Of gas-shells dropping softly behind.

Gas! Gas! Quick, boys! – An ecstasy of fumbling,
10 Fitting the clumsy helmets just in time,
But someone still was yelling out and stumbling
And floundering like a man in fire or lime. –
Dim through the misty panes and thick green light,
As under a green sea, I saw him drowning.
15 In all my dreams, before my helpless sight,
He plunges at me, guttering, choking, drowning.

If in some smothering dreams, you too could pace
Behind the wagon that we flung him in,
And watch the white eyes writhing in his face,
20 His hanging face, like a devil's sick of sin;
If you could hear, at every jolt, the blood
Come gargling from the froth-corrupted lungs,
Obscene as cancer, bitter as the cud
Of vile, incurable sores on innocent tongues, –
25 My friend, you would not tell with such high zest
To children ardent for some desperate glory,
The old Lie: Dulce et decorum est
Pro patria mori.

Wilfred Owen

This poem has a very clear rhyme scheme (*see* Glossary) which is repeated in the second and third stanzas. In the third stanza, however, there are an additional four lines. The important thing to note is that these are 'full rhymes', or 'perfect rhymes'. In other words, the rhyming words are exact rhymes, for example: 'sacks/backs; sludge/trudge; boots/hoots'. If I were writing about how this type of poem works with its definite rhyme scheme, however, I'd want to say something very detailed because its purpose and effect are significant in contributing to the overall meaning. Work through the following tasks to explore this further.

Thinking and writing

1 Make a list of words and phrases in each stanza of 'Dulce et Decorum est' which are negative/critical. Look for examples with hard/harsh sounds to them (lots of consonants) and which paint vivid pictures.

2 Based on your list of the above, explain how Owen describes war.

3 Based on what you have just described, comment on how you think perfect rhyme fits in with this message about war.

4 *Dulce et decorum est pro patria mori* means it is sweet and noble to die for one's country. How might a perfect rhyme seem to fit in with this statement?

When Owen wrote this poem, he was very aware of how the patriotic people at home in Britain might think that it was sweet and noble to fight and die in a distant war. He wanted to describe the truth, though, so that people didn't just believe such rousing Latin phrases. What Owen's poem does is take this heroic-sounding phrase and blow it to pieces by the graphic and horrible descriptions. When you read the poem, all you hear are these graphic and horrifying descriptions, not the perfect-sounding rhyme. In this way Owen uses rhyme for a particular reason. It mirrors the message of the poem. The phrase to describe this is 'the **medium** mirrors the message':

- *Message:* Latin phrase 'sweet and noble' image of war vs. Graphic and horrible description of the reality of war

- *Medium:* Full, perfect rhyme vs. Hard/harsh sounds of the description.

Thinking and writing

Try to sum up the above explanations in a paragraph of your own. Explain why Owen's use of rhyme (as a medium) is so important to the poem's overall meaning (message).

Para-rhyme

Another type of rhyme is called **para-rhyme**, or half rhyme. This is not as perfect and harmonious as full rhyme. This kind of rhyming is usually made by matching consonant rather than vowel sounds. Wilfred Owen has used this rhyme scheme in 'Arms and the Boy'.

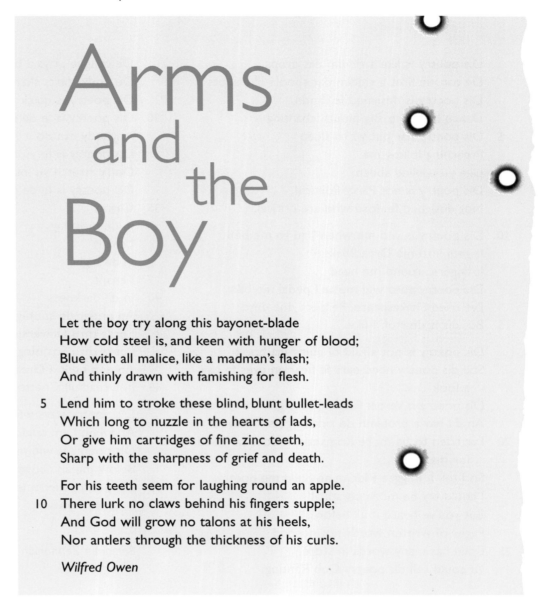

Arms and the Boy

Let the boy try along this bayonet-blade
How cold steel is, and keen with hunger of blood;
Blue with all malice, like a madman's flash;
And thinly drawn with famishing for flesh.

5 Lend him to stroke these blind, blunt bullet-leads
Which long to nuzzle in the hearts of lads,
Or give him cartridges of fine zinc teeth,
Sharp with the sharpness of grief and death.

For his teeth seem for laughing round an apple.
10 There lurk no claws behind his fingers supple;
And God will grow no talons at his heels,
Nor antlers through the thickness of his curls.

Wilfred Owen

Thinking and discussion

1 Note the para-rhymes 'blade/blood, flash/flesh', and so on in 'Arms and the Boy'. Write a few sentences on what sounds are being rhymed in these couplets. Comment on whether they are hard or soft sounds.

2 We have learned Owen's views on war from his poem 'Dulce et Decorum est'. Assuming his attitude is the same in this poem, why does he use para-rhymes to help describe how a young boy should not have to fight with weapons?

Rhythm
Performance poetry

The next element in a particular type of poetry is introduced by Benjamin Zephaniah's 'Dis Poetry'.

Dis Poetry

Dis poetry is like a riddim dat drops
De tongue fires a riddim dat shoots like shots
Dis poetry is designed fe rantin
Dance hall style, Big mouth chanting.
5   Dis poetry nar put yu to sleep
Preaching follow me
Like yu is blind sheep,
Dis poetry is not Party Political
Not designed fe dose who are critical.

10   Dis poetry is wid me when I gu to me bed
It gets into me Dreadlocks
It lingers around me head
Dis poetry goes wid me as I pedal me bike
I've tried Shakespeare, Respect due dere
15   But dis is de stuff I like.

Dis poetry is not afraid of going ina book
Still dis poetry need ears fe hear an eyes fe hav
      a look
Dis poetry is Verbal Riddim, no big words involved
An if I hav a problem de riddim gets it solved,
20   I've tried to be more Romantic, it does nu good
      for me
So I tek a Reggae Riddim an build me poetry,
I could try be more personal
But you've heard it all before,
Pages of written words not needed
25   Brain has many words in store,
Yu could call dis poetry Dub Ranting

De tongue plays a beat
De body starts skanking,
Dis poetry is quick an childish
30   Dis poetry is fe de wise an foolish,
Anybody can do it fe free,
Dis poetry is fe yu an me,
Don't stretch yu imagination
Dis poetry is fe de good of de Nation,
35   Chant,
In de morning
I chant
In de night
I chant
40   In de darkness
An under de spotlight,
I pass thru University
I pass thru Sociology
An den I got a Dread degree
45   In Dreadfull Ghettology.

Dis poetry stays wid me when I run or walk
An when I am talking to meself in poetry I talk,
Dis poetry is wid me,
Below me an above,
50   Dis poetry's from inside me
It goes to yu
WID LUV.

Benjamin Zephaniah

Thinking and discussion

1   What is the main poetic element being demonstrated in 'Dis Poetry'?

2   Benjamin Zephaniah writes poetry that is intended to be read aloud. He is a popular performer of his own work. How do the rhythms of this poem help it to be read aloud?

3   The poem is written in four stanzas of different lengths. How many full stops are in each stanza? What might this tell you about the way it should be read?

John Cooper-Clarke, another performance poet, combines rhythm and rhyme in his poem 'i wanna be yours' to create similar effects.

i wanna be yours

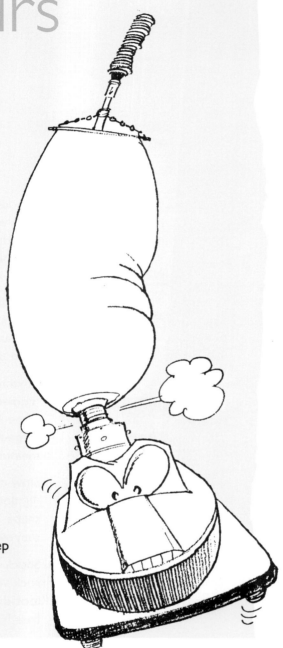

let me be your vacuum cleaner
breathing in your dust
let me be your ford cortina
i will never rust
5   if you like your coffee hot
let me be your coffee pot
you call the shots
i wanna be yours

let me be your raincoat
10   for those frequent rainy days
let me be your dreamboat
you wanna sail away
let me be your teddy bear
take me with you anywhere
15   i don't care
i wanna be yours

let me be your electric meter
i will not run out
let me be the electric heater
20   you get cold without
let me be your setting lotion
hold your hair
with deep devotion
deep as the deep
25   atlantic ocean
that's how deep is my emotion
deep deep deep deep de deep deep
i don't wanna be hers
i wanna be yours

John Cooper-Clarke

Thinking and writing

1 Is 'i wanna be yours' a serious love poem or not? Give reasons to support your views.

2 Make a note of any 'bad' rhymes in this poem (look back to 'Poem in Blank Rhyme' by Glynn Maxwell).

3 Write a sentence on how you think the unsteady rhythms in lines 26–9 might help to deliver the poem's overall message.

Listen carefully to the orchestrated use of rhyme in rhythm in Linton Kwesi Johnson's poem 'Reggae Sounds'.

Reggae Sounds

Shock-black bubble-doun-beat bouncing
rock-wise tumble-doun sound music;
foot-drop find drum, blood story,
bass history is a moving
        is a hurting black story.

5 Thunda from a bass drum sounding
lightening from a trumpet and a organ,
bass and rhythm and trumpet double-up,
team up with drums for a deep doun searching.

Rhythm of a tropical electrical storm
10 (cooled doun to the pace of the struggle),
flame-rhythm of historically yearning
flame-rhythm of the time of turning,
measuring the time for bombs and for burning.

Slow drop. make stop. move forward.
15 dig doun to the root of the pain;
shape it into violence for the people,
they will know what to do, they will do it.

Shock-black bubble-doun-beat bouncing
rock-wise tumble-doun sound music;
20 foot-drop find drum, blood story,
bass history is a moving
        is a hurting black story.

Linton Kwesi Johnson

Activity

In pairs or small groups, prepare and present a reading or make a recording of one of these last three poems. Try to emphasise the use of rhyme and rhythm. It might be appropriate to provide a musical accompaniment to Johnson's 'Reggae Sounds'.

The medium and the message

To draw together some of these observations on the use of rhyme and rhythm in poetry it is appropriate to look at the poem, 'The Buddha's Wife', by Ruth Silcock. In this poem, both of these elements are instrumental in shaping its meaning – the medium mirrors the message in a number of ways:

The Buddha's Wife

It can't have been fun for the Buddha's wife,
Left on her own for the rest of her life
When her good lord fled
The royal bed
5   To seek for his own perfection.

It's said in praise of Mahatma Gandhi –
A sort of saint, though his legs were bandy,
He was skinny and quaint – but still, a saint –
That for years he had nothing to do with his wife:
10   What about her life?

Christian women wear hats in church,
For fear lest their worshipping husbands lurch
And stagger and stare
At the sight of their hair,
15   Shining and heavy and long and free;
'Christian women shall not tempt me',
Said stern St. Paul, who refused to fall
Twice over, and made all women cover
Their burning and moving hair.

20   'Come,' said the milkmaids, 'come, come, come',
To their lord, Lord Krishna; who will not come.
The milkmaids dance and cry to the dawn,
White milk, white flowers on an emerald lawn,
The milkmaids call and the tired cows yawn
25   And nobody comes.

According to men, God has chosen men
To be his voice, his hand, his pen,
To utter his laws, to touch his grace,
To write his books, to read his face,
30   To be his channel to everyone human
Except a woman.

Ruth Silcock

This is a poem about the way women are or have been treated badly by men throughout history and in different cultures. Ruth Silcock takes us through her different illustrations of this by using rhyme and rhythm to create various tones of voice.

A brief summary of the poem would go like this:

1st and 2nd stanzas
The wives of famous, religious men have been ignored by their husbands (who should set good examples of behaviour).

3rd stanza
Women had to wear hats in church so that they didn't look attractive to men in such a place, although St Paul, who made this rule, had obviously found them attractive on more than one occasion!

4th stanza
Loving women called for their Lord Krishna, but, being a typical man, he ignored them.

5th stanza
God is obviously a man and therefore the world should be controlled by men!

Thinking and discussion

1   The first two stanzas of 'The Buddha's Wife' have a rhyme and rhythm commonly found in limericks which are a form of comic verse. What kind of tone does this create and how would the reader react to this at this point?

2   Look closely at lines 16–18. The rhythm is disrupted here, particularly with the enjambement (*see* Glossary and Chapter 2 page 45) in lines 17–18. How does this change the tone from the first two stanzas?

3   The fourth stanza uses slow, steady rhythms and soft assonantal rhymes (*see* Glossary). What effect could this have on the reader at this point in the poem?

4   Look closely at the punctuation in the final stanza. How does this effect the rhythm? How would you speak these lines? Are these soft or hard statements being made?

5   In what ways does the fourth stanza provide a contrast to the fifth?

Activity
Prepare and present a reading or make a recording of 'The Buddha's Wife' which brings out all of the above points.

Forms

There are many types of poems and they come in all shapes and sizes. There is the **'narrative** poem' (**epics** and **ballads**) which essentially tells a story. There is the 'lyric poem' (**haikus**, **elegies** and **odes**) which is essentially musical and provides an intense focus on a particular subject. There is 'free verse' which can be quite random and of which the American poet Robert Frost said 'I'd as soon write free verse as play tennis with the net down!'

Many poems will have a particular form and this is often determined by their use of rhyme or rhythm. The sonnet, for example, traditionally has a set rhyme scheme, and blank verse has a set rhythmic pattern. Most modern poetry does not conform to a particular 'type' but may still have very clear structures and contain set rhyming and rhythms.

The sonnet

One of the most common poetic forms, both historically and in contemporary writing, is the sonnet. The reason for using this form could simply be tradition – that is the style in which everyone wrote at the time. There is, however, a logic to the sonnet form and it is likely that a poet would use it to shape a poem's meaning. Additionally, the discipline of expressing an idea in fourteen lines with a set rhyme pattern provides a creative challenge.

An Italian sonnet requires even greater discipline: a question or idea is posed in the **octave** (first eight lines) and is answered or resolved in the **sestet** (the last six lines).

In a Shakespearean sonnet, each of the three quatrains moves towards a surprising or significant conclusion in the closing rhyming couplet. Two love poems will help illustrate aspects of this development. The first is by Shakespeare (who produced a set of 154 sonnets!) and is Sonnet 116. The second poem is an untitled, modern sonnet by E. E. Cummings.

Sonnet 116

Let me not to the marriage of true minds
Admit impediments. Love is not love
Which alters when it alteration finds,
Or bends with the remover to remove.
5   O, no! it is an ever fixed mark,
That looks on tempests and is never shaken;
It is the star to every wand'ring bark,
Whose worth's unknown, although his height be taken.
Love's not Time's fool, though rosy lips and cheeks
10   Within his bending sickle's compass come;
Love alters not with his brief hours and weeks,
But bears it out even to the edge of doom.
If this be error, and upon me prov'd,
I never writ, nor no man ever lov'd.

William Shakespeare

Thinking and writing

1 Shakespeare's sonnet begins with a premise, an opening argument, that roughly translated means 'I will not accept that anything can get in the way of true love'. ('Let me not to the marriage of true minds/Admit impediments.') List all the lines that support this argument, e.g.

> O no! it is an ever-fixed mark,
> That looks on tempests and is never shaken;

2 How does Shakespeare use the concluding rhyming couplet to round off and complete his argument about true love?

3 Is Shakespeare saying that people are only in love if they never argue, disagree or fall out, however slightly?

(untitled)

it may not always be so;and i say
that if your lips,which i have loved,should touch
another's,and your dear strong fingers clutch
his heart,as mine in time not far away;
5 if on another's face your sweet hair lay
in such a silence as i know,or such
great writhing words as,uttering overmuch,
stand helplessly before the spirit at bay;

if this should be,i say if this should be —
10 you of my heart,send me a little word;
that i may go unto him,and take his hands,
saying,Accept all happiness from me.
Then shall i turn my face,and hear one bird
sing terribly afar in the lost lands.

E. E. Cummings

Thinking and writing

1 E. E. Cummings' argument is that if his loved one should find another person to love as he was loved, then he would wish them both well. Write a few sentences to compare this view with the one expressed in Shakespeare's Sonnet 116.

2 Explain how the last two lines of Cummings' poem suggest a different truth to what was claimed in the first twelve lines.

Whilst these poems are quite different in terms of language and rhyme patterns, they both share one convention of the traditional Shakespearean sonnet: the surprise or significant ending contained in the last two lines. This is something to look for whenever you read and study a sonnet, but it may not always be the case!

Here is another Wilfred Owen poem. 'The Parable of the Old Man and the Young' adds two lines to the sonnet form to make a particular point (again, the medium mirrors the message).

The Parable of the Old Man and the Young

So Abram rose, and clave the wood, and went,
And took the fire with him, and a knife.
And as they sojourned both of them together,
Isaac the first-born spake and said, My Father,
5 Behold the preparations, fire and iron,
But where the lamb for this burnt-offering?
Then Abram bound the youth with belts and straps,
And builded parapets and trenches there,
And stretchèd forth the knife to slay his son.
10 When lo! an angel called him out of heaven,
Saying, Lay not thy hand upon the lad,
Neither do anything to him. Behold,
A ram, caught in a thicket by its horns;
Offer the Ram of Pride instead of him.
15 But the old man would not so, but slew his son,
And half the seed of Europe, one by one.

Wilfred Owen

Thinking and writing

1 Owen's poem is a retelling of the biblical story, or parable, in which Abraham's faith is tested by God. He is told to prove his faith by sacrificing his son Isaac. As he is about to slay his son, and thus prove his faith, God gives him a ram to offer instead. Make a note of the war images that Owen uses as substitute details in his version of this parable.

2 In Owen's version of the story, Abraham does not take up the offer to sacrifice a ram. Had he done so, the poem would have finished at line 14. How does Owen use lines 15–16 to alter the sonnet form and also the ending to this traditional parable?

3 What anti-war message is he delivering?

You can see from Owen's poem that in choosing to write a particular type of poem he has used aspects of the sonnet form for a specific reason, not simply because it is popular.

Writing

The poet Simon Armitage likes to use the sonnet form in his contemporary poems. Read the following two examples and write one paragraph on each explaining how the sonnet form helps him to make his point in the poems.

And if it snowed...

And if it snowed and snow covered the drive
he took a spade and tossed it to one side.
And always tucked his daughter up at night.
And slippered her the one time that she lied.

5 And every week he tipped up half his wage.
And what he didn't spend each week he saved.
And praised his wife for every meal she made.
And once, for laughing, punched her in the face.

And for his mum he hired a private nurse.
10 And every Sunday taxied her to church.
And he blubbed when she went from bad
    to worse.
And twice he lifted ten quid from her purse.

Here's how they rated him when they
    looked back:
sometimes he did this, sometimes he did that.

Simon Armitage

Mice and snakes...

Mice and snakes don't give me the shivers,
which I put down squarely to a decent
    beginning.
Upbringing, I should say, by which I mean
how me and the old man
5 made a good team, and never took
to stepping outside or mixing it up, aside

from the odd time when I had one word too
    many
for my mother, or that underwater evening
when I came home swimming
10 through a quart of stolen home-brewed damson
    wine.

So it goes. And anyway, like he says,
on the day I'm broad and bothered and bold
    enough
to take a swing and try and knock his grin off,

he'll be too old.

Simon Armitage

One of the most common themes presented in the sonnet form is love. Read the following four poems.

Decorated for a
Kiss

I come to her house for love with a basket of red petals.

Men-friend tell me what a fool to go to the girl

Come, man, come fish shark, strong white shark,

At midnight come fish golden snapper along the warm black rocks.

5   But I decide my mind and come to her for love.

Her dress is patterned with blue dragon-flies

She has put a red bead in each ear

Green lizards run in her eyes

Her body has the scent of sun-dried khus-khus grass

10   The sweet fibres she has put between the linen since midday

She has washed her mouth with milk

She has rubbed her lips with bay leaves

She has made her limbs clean with water from a green calabash

Now she offers me a few plums and palm-wine from a gourd of scarlet leather.

Ian McDonald

How do I love thee?

How do I love thee? Let me count
    the ways.
I love thee to the depth and breadth
    and height
My soul can reach, when feeling out
    of sight
For the ends of being and ideal grace.
5 I love thee to the level of every day's
Most quiet need, by sun and candlelight.
I love thee freely, as men strive for right;
I love thee purely, as they turn from praise.
I love thee with the passion put to use
10 In my old griefs, and with my
    childhood's faith.
I love thee with a love I seemed to lose
With my lost saints – I love thee with
    the breath,
Smiles, tears, of all my life! – and, if
    God choose,
I shall but love thee better after death.

Elizabeth Barrett Browning

My love is like to ice

My love is like to ice, and I to fire;
How comes it then that this her cold so great
Is not dissolved through my so hot desire,
But harder grows the more I her entreat?
5 Or how comes it that my exceeding heat
Is not allayed by her heart-frozen cold,
But that I burn much more in boiling sweat,
And feel my flames augmented manifold?
What more miraculous thing may be told,
10 That fire, which all things melts, should harden ice,
And ice, which is congealed with senseless cold,
Should kindle fire by wonderful device?
Such is the power of love in gentle mind,
That it can alter all the course of kind.

Edmund Spenser

IF I PROFANE

	ROMEO	[*To Juliet*] If I profane with my unworthiest hand,
		This holy shrine, the gentle fine is this:
		My lips, two blushing pilgrims, ready stand
		To smooth that rough touch with a tender kiss.
5	JULIET	Good pilgrim, you do wrong your hand too much,
		Which mannerly devotion shows in this;
		For saints have hands that pilgrims' hands do touch,
		And palm to palm is holy palmers' kiss.
	ROMEO	Have not saints lips, and holy palmers too?
10	JULIET	Ay, pilgrim, lips that they must use in pray'r.
	ROMEO	O, then, dear saint, let lips do what hands do!
		They pray; grant thou, lest faith turn to despair.
	JULIET	Saints do not move, though grant for prayers' sake.
	ROMEO	Then move not while my prayer's effect I take. [*Kisses her.*]

William Shakespeare

Writing

Choose one of the love sonnets in this section that you particularly like. Write three or four paragraphs to show how its language and structure helps to shape its overall meaning. There are activities in later chapters to help you with extended writing tasks similar to this but they involve writing about more than one poem. The following is an example of what you could write. It selects Browning's poem so you will have to choose another!

Sample paragraphs

> I like the way the title asks the question 'How do I love thee?' and then uses the poem to answer this.
>
> In this poem there is a perfect balance in the opening line where the first five words are 'How do I love thee?' and the next five are 'Let me count the ways'. This iambic pentameter seems to suggest that there is an obvious answer to the opening question because the line is so perfectly structured. The second line (like all fourteen, an iambic pentameter) continues the steady rhythm which makes everything said sound certain and absolute. It also sums up the love by saying it covers the depth and breadth and height which is everything that can be loved by a person.
>
> The main power of the poem and the way it gets its message across is through the repetition of the three words 'I love thee'. This is repeated seven times (with the word 'love' actually used nine times). Such a repetition of this phrase and the word 'love' leaves the reader in no doubt what this poem is about! The final powerful statement is contained in the last two lines, particularly: 'I shall love thee better after death'. Perhaps this is exaggerating the strength of her love, but that is the whole point of this poem: the love being talked about is bigger and stronger than any other love.

Free verse

Free verse is poetry which does not necessarily follow a particular structure or form. It may still have a structure or form but not necessarily a traditional or conventional one. What it doesn't set out to do is to have a regular rhyme or rhythm (**meter**); free verse uses such elements much more freely and creatively.

The American poet Walt Whitman is considered one of the founders of this type of poetry. The following example, the first of 52 sections from his 'Song of Myself' sequence, demonstrates his flowing lines and interesting use of words:

Song of Myself

I celebrate myself, and sing myself,
And what I assume you shall assume,
For every atom belonging to me as good belongs to you.

I loafe and invite my soul,
5   I lean and loafe at my ease observing a spear of summer grass.

My tongue, every atom of my blood, form'd from this soil, this air,
Born here of parents born here from parents the same, and their
   parents the same,
I, now thirty-seven years old in perfect health begin,
Hoping to cease not till death.
10 Creeds and schools in abeyance,
Retiring back a while suffced at what they are, but never forgotten,
I harbor for good or bad, I permit to speak at every hazard,
Nature without check with original energy.

Walt Whitman

What at first appears to be a random set of lines can be seen, with careful study, to shape meaning in the same way that a sonnet shapes meaning. Adrian Mitchell's poem 'The One About Fred Astaire' does this in a neatly comic way.

Fred Astaire was famous for dancing, particularly tap dancing and Hollywood movie dance routines, and Mitchell's poem uses its structure to mimic the movements of Astaire dancing.

The One About
Fred
Astaire

```
                        No
           it's
              not so much
                    how
  5   he
           moves so much
                 so much
                    as how he
                       stops

 10   and then moves so
           much again all
              over
                 every
                    anywhere
 15              all over
                    so much

      thank you
      Mister Astaire


                       so much

      Adrian Mitchell
```

When reading the following extract from Timothy Emlyn Jones' poem '...pass...', look at how he uses a particular structure to mimic a game of football.

```
. . . . pass pass pass pass pass pass pass pass pass pass run pass
pass pass pass pass pass pass pass pass pass pass  run pass pass
pass pass pass pass pass pass pass pass pass run faster run pass
fast faster go kick go past run run shoot (shoot) oh oooh kick
5   pass pass pass (pass)
                        pass
                            pass
                                pass
                                to the left
10  pass                                (left)
            pass to the centre pass              pass
                                oh
    come up
                come up on the outside
15                              run
    come

            come
                    come my darling
    come gentle
20          here
                (here)
                in ease
                        pass the winter's sun

    easy
25      ease the ball
                    stall
                    watch for the moment
                                    toe it turn
                                            ease the moment

30  seize the instant
                    shoot

    an arc of grace sprung high
                    the sun its keystone
    shaping a shimmering vault
35                              a canopy of prayer and delight
                                a drift of sky
                                    arena of flight
                                a cathedral of play
                                    of tribal rite


Timothy Emlyn Jones
```

Thinking and discussion

1 How does Jones use two styles of type to indicate different descriptions of a football match?

2 Comment on how effectively you feel this structure captures the actual playing of a football game.

Wrap it up

You have explored many types of poems and seen how rhyme and rhythm or particular forms are used to shape meaning and add variety and interest for the reader. The work of Wilfred Owen provides ample evidence of how the type of poem being written makes a major impact on its ability to put across its meaning: the medium mirrors the message. You have seen how types of poetry as diverse as a Shakespeare sonnet or Adrian Mitchell's free verse deserve to be studied closely to appreciate their purpose and effect. In the following chapters that look at annotating and then comparing pairs of poems, you will be able to apply your knowledge and understanding of how different types of poems work. You will support this with your appreciation of how tone and the use of poetic techniques contribute to a poem's overall meaning. The 'Three Ts' are hopefully the launch-pad for your more pleasurable and informed journey through the reading and study of poetry to come in this book and beyond.

Annotating poetry

When studying poetry and writing about it, you will, inevitably, need to make detailed notes about poems. One of the best ways to do this is to write on a copy of the poem itself or to make notes on a separate sheet of paper which are keyed to the lines of the poem. These annotations should be seen as explorations of, and collections from, the text you are reading.

You explore by asking questions and reacting to what you read. If you don't understand a word or an image you should ask questions about it. This then becomes a reminder that there are answers (or helpful hints) which need to be found! Reacting immediately to what you read can register important first impressions (for example, when beginning to hear the tone of a poem).

You collect ideas and information as you read to build up a greater picture and understanding of a poem. If you do not collect something when you first notice it, you might lose it! If, at the end, you want to reject ideas and information you can simply draw a line through these.

The following two poems, 'Malta' by Helen Dunmore and 'Between the Lines' by Carole Satyamurti, are annotated as examples of this process. 'Malta' has annotations on the poem itself and 'Between the Lines' has accompanying annotations. Of course, you can usually only make annotations on the poem itself if you have a photocopy.

The other time you will annotate on the page is when you are studying an anthology of poems for a particular exam. The kinds of annotations you will do for this will be quite different. The ones we are looking at in *this* chapter are the detailed explorations and collections which help you to appreciate and understand a particular poem. In an anthology you will want 'lighter' annotations: reminders of overall meaning, links between poems and occasional references to specific features. There is a danger in over-annotating in such anthologies. This can lead to reliance on notes rather than responding to specific questions. In turn, this can produce simple regurgitation of information rather than engaging with the poem and question in a fresh and lively way.

The following two poems look at the tensions created when parents are over-protective of their children. Such attempts at protection can lead to ignorance, resentment and rejection. We are not studying these attitudes in themselves but, as a pair, they do make an excellent set of companion poems. You might like to think about their similarities and differences, particularly in considering where the poets direct their sympathies.

The annotations written on these poems were both produced by 15-year-old students and represent their initial thoughts and ideas.

Annotating on the poem

Malta

negative opening tone

The sea's a <u>featureless</u> blaze.
On photographs nothing comes out
but glare, with that scarlet-rimmed fishing boat
<u>far-off</u>, <u>lost</u> to the lens.

why featureless?

why far off lost?

5   At noon a <u>stiff-legged</u> tourist in shorts
steps, camera poised. He's <u>stilted</u>
as a flamingo, <u>pink-limbed</u>.

man is uncomfortable, out of place

Icons of Malta gather around him.
He sweats as a procession passes
10   and women with <u>church-dark</u> faces
brush him as if he were air.

negative image man is rejected

introduces daughter aged 12

He holds a white crocheted dress
to give to his twelve-year-old daughter
who moons in the apartment, sun-sore.
15   The sky's <u>tight as a drum</u>, <u>hard</u>
to breathe in, <u>hard to walk under</u>.

more negative images

He would not buy 'bikini for daughter'
though the man pressed him, with plump fingers
spreading out scraps of blue cotton.

why won't he buy the bikini? Is he mean?

his wife rejects him like women in 3rd stanza

20   <u>Let her stay young, let her know nothing</u>.
Let her body remain skimpy and sudden.
His wife <u>builds arches of silence over her
new breasts</u> and packets of <u>tampons</u> marked
      'slender'.
At nights, when they think she's asleep,
25   they ache in the same places
but never louder than a whisper.

Answer to questions above? He wants to protect her?

girl is growing up?

man is an outsider, he watches

He watches more women melt into a porch.
Their white, still laundry flags from window
      to window
while they are <u>absent</u>, their balconies <u>blank</u>.

more negative images

do we dislike the father or feel sympathy for him?

30   At six o'clock, when he comes home and snicks
his key in the lock so softly neither will catch it
he hears one of them laugh.
They are <u>secret</u> in the kitchen, talking of nothing,
strangers whom anyone might love.

do they laugh at him? why?

Helen Dunmore

Annotating on a separate sheet

BETWEEN THE LINES

Words were dust-sheets, blinds.
People dying randomly, for 'want of breath',
shadowed my bed-times.
Babies happened;
5 adults buried questions under bushes.

Nouns would have been too robust
for body-parts; they were
curt, homeless prepositions—'inside',
'down there', 'behind', 'below'. No word
10 for what went on in darkness, overheard.

Underground, straining for language
that would let me out, I pressed to the radio,
read forbidden books. And once
visited Mr Cole. His seventeen
15 budgerigars praised God continually.

He loved all words, he said, though he used
few to force a kiss. All that summer
I longed to ask my mother, starved myself,
prayed, imagined skirts were getting tight,
20 hoped jumping down ten stairs would put it right.

My parents fought in other rooms,
their tight-lipped murmuring muffled
by flock wallpaper.
What was wrong, what they had to say
25 couldn't be shared with me.

He crossed the threshold in a wordless
slam of doors. 'Gone to live near work'
my mother said, before she tracked down
my diary, broke the lock, made me cut out
30 pages that guessed what silence was about.

Carole Satyamurti

Keying your comments to the stanzas and lines

1st stanza

Line 1 – opening metaphor – suggests covering or hiding things?

Lines 2–5 – more images of concealing things: 'want of breath' and 'buried ... under bushes'.

2nd stanza

Focus on language here – 'nouns' and 'prepositions' (links back to 'words').

Lines 8–9 – words/phrases put in single quotation marks to indicate polite (but still secret/deceptive?) ways of saying things.

Line 7 – 'body-parts' to mean sexual parts?

3rd stanza

Line 11 – continued reference to 'language'.

Line 12 – introduced to 'I', person in the poem.

Lines 12–13 – listens to 'radio' and reads 'forbidden books' for information/knowledge about things being concealed.

Lines 14–15 – who is 'Mr Cole'? What about 'budgerigars'? Don't get this.

4th stanza

Line 16 – more on 'words'. Mr Cole uses them to kiss girl – persuades/tricks her?
(Is he just an older man she has met?)

Lines 18–20 – girl imagines skirts getting tight and jumps downstairs to 'put it right' – thinks she's pregnant? Trying to get rid of baby?

5th stanza

More on concealing things: 'tight-lipped'.

Parents don't share with the child.

6th stanza

Father leaves home? Doesn't say anything: a 'wordless/slam of doors'.

Mother still tells lies: 'Gone to live near work'.

Lines 28–30 – final nasty detail: mother tears up diary entries the child has made to try and explain things for herself.

You can see from the annotations both on the poem and as an attached sheet, there are many questions that still need answering. It is by answering these, that the real understanding starts to take shape. These detailed annotations you have made provide a framework for your further study.

Activity

Here is another poem about the tense relationships within a family for you to annotate as an exercise. This is a deceptively simple poem so read it carefully twice before you begin making your notes. It is a poem about how both anger and love can exist in a family at the same time.

Do your annotations on a separate sheet of paper and key it simply by using stanza and/or line numbers.

MY SON WANTS TO RIDE THE CHAIRLIFT

```
    my son wants to ride the chairlift
    up the snowless ski run
    and i'm elected to accompany him.

    i'm terrified,
5   especially when i discover
    that i can't fasten our car-type safety belt
    without adjusting it.

    "hang on!" i caution: "don't lean forward!"
    and just then my wife and daughter
10  start yelling for us to face them
    so they can snap our pictures.

    "ignore them!" i gasp,
    and i stare rigidly upwards.
    but they won't stop yelling.
15  what infuriates me, i think,
    is that women so often assume
    the fears of men to be ridiculous.
    they tease me while, in my terror and incompetence,
    i hold my son's life in jeopardy.
```

20   back on the ground, legs shaky,
     i make a point of telling them
     that i was not amused.
     now my daughter feels hurt and guilty.
     and my wife won't talk.
25   i'm still so shaken,
     driving down the mountain,
     that at one point.
     turning back from a short cut
     that turned out not to be,
30   i almost back us off a cliff.

     back on the still treacherous main road,
     i glance in the rear-view mirror
     at my youngest child,
     less than a year,
35   asleep in her car seat,
     and my eyes are all but blinded by tears.

     the official version will be
     that my uptightness has spoiled another day.

     Gerald Locklin

Companion poems

It can be a challenging, as a well as a rewarding, activity to compare and contrast poems with a common theme. Their shared subject-matter can capture your interest, while analysing and evaluating their differing viewpoints can help you to explore the meaning of each poem in depth.

One of the key assessment objectives of GCSE English Literature, where the study of poetry is such an important element, is that candidates must demonstrate their ability to *explore relationships and comparisons within and between texts, and to select and evaluate relevant material*. In GCSE English, where the study of poetry is also important, there is a similar commitment to make comparisons as students must demonstrate an ability to *select material appropriate to their purpose, to collate material from different sources, and to make cross references*. These will be essential features of coursework and examination questions. This chapter on 'Companion poems' is designed to help you develop the necessary skills.

When first reading each poem, remember to apply the 'Three Ts' (Tone, Techniques, Type), as outlined in Chapters 1 to 3 of this book. You should do this when annotating each poem (as outlined in Chapter 4) either directly onto a copy of the poem, or as keyed notes on a separate sheet of paper.

All of the pairs of poems in this section are related to one another by theme. Some are selected for their strong similarities and some for their clearly contrasting views and these are aspects which must be distinguished when making comparisons. They are also provided to extend your reading of a wide range of poems.

Blind faith?

The first pair of companion poems is Roger McGough's 'Waving at Trains' and U. A. Fanthorpe's 'Patience Strong'. The notes which follow the poems are provided as a *model* for the focus and attention you should give when making comparisons between these and other poems in this chapter.

Waving at Trains

Do people who wave at trains
Wave at the driver, or at the train itself?
Or, do people who wave at trains
Wave at the passengers? Those hurtling strangers,
5   The unidentifiable flying faces.

They must think we like being waved at.
Children do perhaps, and alone
In a compartment, the occasional passenger
Who is himself a secret waver at trains.
10   But most of us are unimpressed.

Some even think they're daft.
Stuck out there in a field, grinning.
But our ignoring them, our blank faces,
Even our pulled tongues and up you signs
15   Come three miles further down the line.

Out of harm's way by then
They continue their walk.
Refreshed and made pure, by the mistaken belief
That their love has been returned,
20   Because they have not seen it rejected.

It's like God in a way. Another day
Another universe. Always off somewhere.
And left behind, the faithful few,
Stuck out there. Not a care in the world.
25   All innocence. Arms in the air. Waving.

Roger McGough

PATIENCE STRONG

Everyone knows her name. Trite calendars
Of rose-nooked cottages or winding ways
Display her sentiments in homespun verse
Disguised as prose. She has her tiny niche
5 In women's magazines, too, tucked away
Among the recipes or near the end
Of some perennial serial. Her theme
Always the same: rain falls in every life,
But rainbows, bluebirds, spring, babies or God
10 Lift up our hearts. No doubt such rubbish sells.
She must be feathering her inglenook.
Genuine poets seldom coin the stuff,
Nor do they flaunt such aptly bogus names.
Their message is oblique; it doesn't fit
15 A pocket diary's page; nor does it pay.

One day in epileptic out-patients,
A working-man, a fellow in his fifties,
Was feeling bad. I brought a cup of tea.
He talked about his family and job:
20 His dad was in the Ambulance Brigade;
He hoped to join, but being epileptic,
They wouldn't have him. *Naturally*, he said,
With my disease, I'd be a handicap.
But I'd have liked to help. He sucked his tea,
25 Then from some special inner pocket brought
A booklet muffled up in cellophane,
Unwrapped it gently, opened at a page –
Characteristic cottage garden, seen
Through chintzy casement windows. Underneath
30 Some cosy musing in the usual vein,
And *See*, he said, *this is what keeps me going.*

U. A. Fanthorpe

A model for comparing poems

'Waving at Trains'

1 By tracing the tone of the poem, 'Waving at Trains', through the five stanzas, you have a choice of tones. You either feel that the drive through the five stanzas is towards a mocking and dismissive tone or that by the fifth stanza there is a shift and the development of an appreciative and sympathetic tone.

Stanza	Tone
1	A series of genuine, innocent questions?
2	Beginning to show impatience with train wavers?
3	Showing outright hostility towards train wavers?
4	Being a little condescending towards train wavers?
5	Still scathing, or is there a new appreciation/understanding?

2 Making a decision on the tone cannot be divorced from an understanding of the poem's overall meaning. Is this really a poem about people who wave at trains? The final stanza suggests that they are in fact used as a metaphor to represent people who believe in God. The passengers in the train ignore the train wavers and thus do not acknowledge their existence in the same way that God does not, apparently, speak to and thus acknowledge the believer's existence. If this is the poem's overall meaning, you might decide that the poem therefore has a cynical tone. However, how do the train wavers feel when they are waving? The poem tells us they have 'Not a care in the world', they are 'All innocence'. This suggests contentment. With this view of the poem's overall meaning you might believe that the poem has a sympathetic and understanding tone.

3 In terms of techniques, this poem is quite straightforward. The most obvious poetic devices are the use of questions in the first stanza to set the poem up, and then in the final stanza some short and simple sentences slow the pace and give certainty to the message that the train wavers are at least content and happy in their roles.

4 The comparison of the train and its passengers with God, 'It's like God in a way', gives the poem a deeper meaning. This simile transforms the questions into a reflection on God's relationship with creation and the nature of faith.

5 As a type of poem, this is neatly structured into five stanzas with each one presenting a particular view and focus. The first four stanzas focus on the train wavers so that in the fifth, the sudden shift in focus to 'God' is highlighted.

'Patience Strong'

6 There are two main tones with a definite shift from one to the other. In the first stanza, Fanthorpe is comparing herself as a writer with Patience Strong (the person who writes the pulp, sentimental verse in greetings cards). She describes Patience Strong and her writing as 'trite', 'homespun verse', 'tiny niche' and 'rubbish'. Her tone appears to be contemptuous. Having rubbished Patience Strong's writing

and her apparently sentimental messages of 'rain falls in every life,/But rainbows, bluebirds, spring, babies or God/Lift up our hearts', Fanthorpe discovers another view to this. In the second stanza she relates the story of meeting an epileptic in an out-patients clinic who finds comfort in the sentimental messages of people like Patience Strong. The tone here has shifted dramatically to one of sympathy and understanding, similar to the shift which occurs in McGough's poem. Fanthorpe's shift in tone is sincere because where she was previously so scathing, she now has the honesty to accept that this type of writing can have a purpose.

7   The use of techniques in this poem is also straightforward. It uses the recurring image of the 'rose-nooked cottages' to provide a focus for the surprise of discovering substance and value beneath this surface beauty. The image is extended in the first section with the metaphoric joke about Strong 'feathering her inglenook' (meaning she makes lots of money, i.e. feathering her nest), and in the second section it is picked up with the line 'Characteristic cottage garden, seen/Through chintzy casement windows'. Throughout the poem there is the use of negative language to refer to Strong and her writing. This makes Fanthorpe's change of heart all the more surprising and dramatic and is thus a simple but effective device.

8   As a type of poem there is no set conventional form, but there is an important structure in the symmetry of the two stanzas: both are of equal length, with the first condemning/criticising Strong and the second recognising/supporting her value to some people.

Comparison

9   Both poems can be seen to have many similarities. They are both about faith and belief. In each poem, the writer is initially cynical but, by the end, comes to an understanding (although you may feel this is less strong with McGough's poem). They are both direct with their language and use simple techniques to convey their messages. Whilst having differing structures (one has five stanzas of equal length, the other has two) they both work through these to develop and change their attitude and tone of voice.

In a fuller response, you would add much more detail. For example, you should compare the negative language and images contained in both poems by referring to specific examples. Each poem tells a story and creates, to varying degrees, recognisable characters that should be described.

What I have said above is *my* interpretation and is open to challenge. You could argue that both writers remain critical. As long as you can support your view with clear arguments and reference to examples, you are entitled (and indeed encouraged) to have your own opinions and interpretations.

The following sets of companion poems are given to provide further practice in comparing and contrasting. If appropriate, any set could be used for a coursework assignment. If used for this purpose, remember to annotate them closely and apply the 'Three Ts'. In the models above, we focused our attention mainly on tone. When referring to any specific techniques in the following poems, always comment on their purpose and effect. The two poems already looked at did not follow a traditional form (although they were carefully structured) nor did they make particular use of rhyme and rhythm. Remember to consider whether there are any elements that need comment and analysis in the types of poems presented in the following sets.

What's love got to do with it?

the SEDUCTION

A clumsy poem of teenage angst!!!

After the party, early Sunday morning.
He led her to the quiet bricks of Birkenhead docks.
Far past the silver stream of traffic through the city.
Far from the blind windows of the tower blocks.

5   He sat down in the darkness, leather jacket creaking madly.
He spat into the river, fumbled in a bag.
He handed her the vodka, and she knocked it back like water.
He giggled, drunk and nervous, and he muttered 'little slag'.

She had met him at the party, and he'd danced with her all night.
10 He'd told her about football, Sammy Lee and Ian Rush.
She had nodded, quite enchanted, and her eyes were wide and bright
As he enthused about the Milk Cup, and the next McGuigan fight.

As he brought her more drinks, so she fell in love
With his eyes as blue as iodine,
15 With the fingers that stroked her neck and her thighs
And the kisses that tasted of nicotine.

Then: 'I'll take you to the river where I spend the afternoons,
When I should be at school, or eating me dinner.
Where I go, by myself, with me dad's magazines
20 And a bag filled with shimmering, sweet paint thinner.'

So she followed him there, all high white shoes,
All wide blue eyes, and bottles of vodka.
And sat in the dark, her head rolling forward
Towards the frightening scum on the water.

25   And talked about school, in a disjointed way:
      About O-levels she'd be sitting in June.
      She chattered on, and stared at the water,
      The Mersey, green as a septic wound.

      Then, when he swiftly contrived to kiss her
30   His kiss was scented by Listerine
      And she stifled a giggle, reminded of numerous
      Stories from teenage magazines ...

      When she discovered she was three months gone
      She sobbed in the cool, locked darkness of her room
35   And she ripped up all her *My Guy* and her *Jackie* photo-comics
      Until they were just bright paper, like confetti, strewn

      On the carpet. And on that day, she broke the heels
      Of her high white shoes (as she flung them at the wall).
      And realised, for once, that she was truly truly frightened
40   But more than that, cheated by the promise of it all.

      For where, now, was the summer of her sixteenth year;
      Full of the glitzy fashion features, and stories of romance?
      Where a stranger could lead you to bright new worlds,
      And how would you know, if you never took a chance?

45   Full of glossy horoscopes, and glamour with a stammer;
      Full of fresh fruit diets – how did she feel betrayed? –
      How, with a softly rounded belly, she was sickened every morning,
      By stupid, stupid promises, only tacitly made.

      Where were the glossy photographs of summer,
50   Day trips to Blackpool, jumping all the rides?
      And where, now, were the pink smiling faces in the picture:
      Three girls paddling in the grey and frothy tide?

      So she cried that she had missed all the innnocence around her
      And all the parties where you meet the boy next door.
55   Where you walk, hand in hand in an acne'd wonderland.
      With a glass of lager-shandy, on a carpeted floor.

      But, then again, better to be smoking scented drugs
      Or festering, invisibly, unemployed.
      Better to destroy your life in modern, man-made ways
60   Than to fall into this despicable, feminine void.

      Better to starve yourself, like a sick, precocious child
      Than to walk through town with a belly huge and ripe.
      And better, now, to turn away, move away, fade away.
      Than to have the neighbours whisper that 'you always looked
        the type'.

      Eileen McAuley

September
Assignment

Write about 500 words on one of the following:
i) My summer holiday
ii) Adolescent relationships
iii) Pop music

Deep in the heat of a camp site rave,
Little Tina Turnbull dances the night,
Filled with the thrill of a chemical wave,
Flying in the flash of fluorescent light.
5   Driven by the rhythm of a high speed laser,
Pulse pumped hard with a pocket full of pills,
High as a kite, sharp as a razor,
Stuttering steps in the strobe light stills.
Boogying close as the beat drives harder,
10 Hippity together to the disco door,
Sinking in the seat of a clapped out Lada,
Scrabbling for the condoms on the cold car floor.
Back to the caravan at half past three
(Parents paralytic on the double divan)
15 Worried over syphilis and HIV,
Pimples that appeared instead of a tan.
Packed next morning sitting in the car,
Eyes shut tight with her walkman on,
Dreams of a foetus in a marmalade jar,
20 Childhood, babies, holidays gone.
Rainclouds form on the fading hill,
Wipers start to squeak on the fly-stained screen,
Eyes turned cold in the wintry chill
As the radio plays sweet little sixteen.

Mike Kivi

Thinking and writing

1   There is much to note about the language of 'The Seduction'. Make a list of all of the negative words and images, e.g. 'slag' and 'The Mersey, green as a septic wound'. How do these contribute to the overall tone?

2   Make a note of the rhyme scheme. Is there a purpose to this? Think of the work on 'Dulce et Decorum est' in Chapter 3.

3   There are many references which date this poem, e.g. 'Sammy Lee', 'McGuigan fight' and 'Jackie'. Make a note of any others and establish when the poem was written. Does this have any effect on the poem's relevance to teenagers today?

4   What is the significance of the opening section of 'September Assignment' printed in italics?

5   The language of this poem is also particularly evocative. List all the negative words and comment on the poem's overall tone.

6   Refer to the work on this poem in Chapter 2 Techniques (*see* page 44). Consider how the rhythms of this poem contribute to its realism.

7   Both poems are about girls who are aged 16. They have had a one-night stand and become pregnant. How does the world (whether their personal world or the world at large) apparently view their predicament?

Persuasion

To His Coy Mistress

Had we but world enough, and time,
This coyness, lady, were no crime.
We would sit down, and think which way
To walk, and pass our long love's day.
5 Thou by the Indian Ganges' side
Should'st rubies find: I by the tide
Of Humber would complain. I would
Love you ten years before the Flood.
And you should, if you please, refuse
10 Till the conversion of the Jews.
My vegetable love should grow
Vaster than empires, and more slow.
An hundred years should go to praise
Thine eyes, and on thy forehead gaze:
15 Two hundred to adore each breast:
But thirty thousand to the rest;
An age at least to every part,
And the last age should show your heart.
For, lady, you deserve this state,
20 Nor would I love at lower rate.
    But at my back I always hear
Time's wingéd chariot hurrying near:
And yonder all before us lie
Deserts of vast eternity.
25 Thy beauty shall no more be found;
Nor, in thy marble vault, shall sound
My echoing song; then worms shall try
That long-preserved virginity,
And your quaint honour turn to dust,

30   And into ashes all my lust.
      The grave's a fine and private place,
      But none, I think, do there embrace.
          Now, therefore, while the youthful hue
      Sits on thy skin like morning dew,
35   And while thy willing soul transpires
      At every pore with instant fires,
      Now let us sport us while we may;
      And now, like amorous birds of prey,
      Rather at once our Time devour,
40   Than languish in his slow-chapt power.
      Let us roll all our strength and all
      Our sweetness up into one ball,
      And tear our pleasures with rough strife
      Through the iron gates of life.
45   Thus, though we cannot make our Sun
      Stand still, yet we will make him run.

Andrew Marvell

An Answer to a Love-Letter

      Is it to me, this sad lamenting strain?
      Are heaven's choicest gifts bestowed in vain?
      A plenteous fortune, and a beauteous bride,
      Your love rewarded, gratify'd your pride:
5   Yet leaving her — 'tis me that you pursue
      Without one single charm, but being new.
      How vile is man! how I detest their ways

Of artful falsehood, and designing praise!

Tasteless, an easy happiness you slight,

10 Ruin your joy, and mischief your delight,

Why should poor pug (the mimic of your kind)

Wear a rough chain, and be to box confin'd?

Some cup, perhaps, he breaks, or tears a fan

While roves unpunish'd the destroyer, man.

15 Not bound by vows, and unrestrain'd by shame,

In sport you break the heart, and rend the fame.

Not that your art can be successful here,

Th'already plunder'd need no robber fear:

Nor sighs, nor charms, nor flatteries can move,

20 Too well secur'd against a second love.

Once, and but once, that devil charm'd my mind;

To reason deaf, to observation blind;

I idly hoped (what cannot love persuade?)

My fondness equal'd, and my love repaid:

25 Slow to distrust, and willing to believe,

Long hush'd my doubts, and did myself deceive;

But oh! too soon – this tale would ever last;

Sleep, sleep my wrongs, and let me think

    them past.

For you, who mourn with counterfeited grief,

30 And ask so boldly like a begging thief,

May soon some other nymph inflict the pain,

You know so well with cruel art to feign.

Though long you sported with Dan Cupid's dart,

You may see eyes, and you may feel a heart.

35 So the brisk wits, who stop the evening coach,

Laugh at the fear which follows their approach;

With idle mirth, and haughty scorn despise

The passenger's pale cheek and staring eyes:

But seiz'd by Justice, find a fright no jest,

40 And all the terror doubled in their breast.

Lady Mary Wortley Montagu

Thinking and discussion

1 'To His Coy Mistress' is a famous, much anthologised poem. It is structured in three clear sections: 'If', 'But' and 'However'.

   In section 1, the poet says that if he had loads of time, he would spend all the time in the world flattering his loved one without expecting her to be with him. That is precisely what he does in this section. He flatters her with exaggerated praise, e.g. his most outrageous chat-up line:

> 'An hundred years should go to praise
> Thine eyes, and on thy forehead gaze:
> Two hundred to adore each breast:
> But thirty thousand to the rest… '

   How would you describe the tone of this section?

2 But there isn't time for all this flattery so in section 2 he tries to terrify his loved one into being with him. What negative language and imagery does he use here to signify the lack of time? Does this alter the tone?

3 In section 3, however, he feels that he can now be reasonable and logical. The first two sections were extremes, so he now presents, for himself, the obvious and rational explanation of the situation. If he is suddenly being reasonable, how does he intend this tone to persuade his loved one to be with him? Is it all a piece of typically calculated and manipulative male behaviour?

4 As a possible riposte to Marvell, 'An Answer to a Love-Letter' knows how to respond to flattery. Such flattery is called 'artful falsehood' and 'designing praise'. What do you think this means?

5 There is a clear criticism of the man not offering marriage in his proposal for love. Can you find this quote?

6 In what ways does Lady Montagu feel that a previous experience makes her immune to the man's suggestions?

The OAP guide to love

Age to Youth

The sooty bush in the park
is green as any forest
for the boy to lie beneath,
with his arms around his dearest;

5   the black of the back street
is washed as any cloud
when the girl and the boy
touch hands among the crowd.

No, nothing's better than love,
10 than to want and to hold:
it is wise in the young
to forget the common world:

to be lost in the flesh
and the light shining there:
15 not to listen to the old
whose tune is fear and care —

who tell them love's a drink
poisoned with sorrow,
the flesh a flower today
20 and withered by tomorrow.

It is wise in the young
to let heart go racing heart,
to believe that the earth
is young and safe and sweet;

25 and the message we should send
from age back to youth
is that every kiss and glance
is truer than the truth;

that whatever we repent
30 of the time that we live,
it is never what we give —
it is never that we love.

Judith Wright

KISSING

The young are walking on the riverbank,
arms around each other's waists and shoulders,
pretending to be looking at the waterlilies
and what might be a nest of some kind, over
5   there, which two who are clamped together
mouth to mouth have forgotten about.
The others, making courteous detours
around them, talk, stop talking, kiss.
They can see no one older than themselves.
10   It's their river. They've got all day.

Seeing's not everything. At this very
moment the middle-aged are kissing
in the backs of taxis, on the way
to airports and stations. Their mouths and tongues
15   are soft and powerful and as moist as ever.
Their hands are not inside each other's clothes
(because of the driver) but locked so tightly
together that it hurts: it may leave marks
on their not of course youthful skin, which they won't
20   notice. They too may have futures.

Fleur Adcock

Thinking and discussion

1 'Age to Youth' is, essentially, a 'wise' message from the old to the young. Is it a positive or negative message? Look closely at the imagery of the first two stanzas where being young is seen to have rather special powers/effects.

2 One of the poem's more difficult lines is in the penultimate stanza: 'truer than the truth'. Crack this one and you are understanding the poem!

3 The poem 'Kissing' has a similar structure to 'Patience Strong': two stanzas of equal line length which present diametrically opposed views. The first is about young lovers; the second about older lovers. What do you notice that is similar about the descriptions but which is being used to make opposing points? One of the key lines in this poem is 'They too have futures'.

Breaking up is hard to do

XXIV

Love, we must part now: do not let it be
Calamitous and bitter. In the past
There has been too much moonlight
   and self-pity:
Let us have done with it: for now at last
5 Never has sun more boldly paced the sky,
Never were hearts more eager to be free,
To kick down worlds, lash forests; you and I
No longer hold them; we are husks, that see
The grain going forward to a different use.

10 There is regret. Always, there is regret.
But it is better that our lives unloose,
As two tall ships, wind-mastered, wet with light,
Break from an estuary with their courses set,
And waving part, and waving drop from sight.

Philip Larkin

First Ice

A girl freezes in a telephone booth.
In her draughty overcoat she hides
A face all smeared
In tears and lipstick.

5 She breathes on her thin palms.
Her fingers are icy. She wears earrings.

She'll have to go home alone, alone,
Along the icy street.

First ice. It is the first time.
10 The first ice of telephone phrases.

Frozen tears glitter on her cheeks —
The first ice of human hurt.

Andrei Voznesensky
(trans. by Stanley Kunitz)

Thinking and writing

1 Philip Larkin's poem, XXIV, presents a positive and hopeful view of lovers parting. How does the image of the parting ships present this positive tone?

2 This is a carefully crafted sonnet. Notice how the opening section presents the argument for the parting and the second section shows how this should be done. Summarise the detail and meaning of both sections.

3 Larkin uses enjambement to place emphasis on key words and phrases, especially in the opening section. Find and comment on the purpose and effect of these.

4 Does the rhyming add any impact to the whole or to parts of this poem?

5 We do not know exactly what has happened to the girl in 'First Ice' but we can guess. What do the clues 'draughty overcoat', 'lipstick', 'earrings' and 'She'll have to go home alone, alone' tell us about the events leading up to her being in the telephone booth?

6 How is the central image of this poem sustained and developed?

7 In what ways are these two poems similar and yet dramatically different?

Fathers and daughters

Almost Communication

My father just passed me
in his Fiat 127
I was cycling my bicycle 'Hideous'.

They stopped at O'Meara's
5   for the *Connacht Tribune*.
As I passed I shouted
'road hog' in the window.

The occupants laughed.

Before this he owned
10   a Renault 12,
we called it
the 'Ballyhaunis cow killer'.

Later we met outside the sister's,
'Wouldn't you think
15   he'd buy you a decent bike, the miser.'

'If he had your money,' I said
and we laughed.

The neighbours with their ears
to the rose bushes
20   think that we're great friends.

I haven't seen his eyes for years.

Rita Ann Higgins

The Laugh

Dad, his moods as black as carbon,
laws intransigent – anthracite
burning slow but then heat, beat,
yell, holler – "Steal, would you?"
5   belt leather on our thinnest skin.
"Lie, would you?" Blue-eyed Dad
boiling up revenge, pouring it out.

Nights I'd dream of it and days too –
of his mouth opening red as a furnace
10   and a laugh issuing, bright yellow.

That day. Black-haired Dad not hailing
neighbours, intent on the slag
beneath, turning it, picking
for coal with thick fingers.
15   Our fingers cold-clumsy picking too,
dropping dark nuggets into the sack,
quiet, saying nothing, watchful . . .
afraid of the hairs on his eyebrows,
the frost in his voice. "Po-lice!"
20   Two syllables hung on air . . . then
up, the pair of us in his iron hands,
chucked in the pram with the half-empty
sack and dour Dad bowling down the heap,
along the hawthorn lane, past the stream,
25   up Colonel's Walk and up Coburg Street,
the pram rattling and rollicking.

That day, eyes slammed, I heard Dad laugh.
The only time. That pure gold like the heart
of the fire. Terrifying.

Jacqueline Brown

Thinking and writing

1 'Almost Communication' is a straightforward and simply structured poem; all of its power is contained in the shock and surprise of the last line. Elaborate on how the rhyme of 'ears/years' helps to achieve this significant ending.

2 'The Laugh' is a poem full of potent images: the black of coal and the red of its burning linked to the father's dark moods and fiery anger. Make a list of these references.

3 In what way is the ending full of irony?

Match of the day

The Catch

Forget
the long, smouldering
afternoon. It is

this moment
5 when the ball scoots
off the edge

of the bat; upwards,
backwards, falling
seemingly

10 beyond him
yet he reaches
and picks it

out
of its loop
15 like

an apple
from a branch,
the first of the season.

Simon Armitage

the perfect match

There is nothing like the five minutes to go:
Your lads one up, your lads one down, or the whole
  Thing even. How you actually feel,
    What you truly know,
5 Is that your lads are going to do it. So,

However many times in the past the fact
Is that they didn't, however you screamed and strained,
  Pummelled the floor, looked up and groaned
    As the Seiko ticked
10 On, when the ultimate ball is nodded or kicked

The man in the air is you. Your beautiful wife
May curl in the corner yawningly calm and true,
  But something's going on with you
    That lasts male life.
15 Love's one thing, but this is the Big Chief.

Glyn Maxwell

Thinking and discussion

These two poems try to catch a moment in sport. Note how the movement of the
words on the page also tries to capture and mirror some of the movement, tension
and excitement of the sporting moments they describe. You could compare these two
poems with the extract from Timothy Emlyn Jones' poem, ' ...pass... ' in Chapter 3 on
Types (*see* page 74).

A calling

The Call

From our low seat beside the fire
  Where we have dozed and dreamed and watched the glow
  Or raked the ashes, stopping so
We scarcely saw the sun or rain
5   Above, or looked much higher
Than this same quiet red or burned-out fire.
     To-night we heard a call,
     A rattle on the window-pane,
     A voice on the sharp air,
10 And felt a breath stirring our hair,
  A flame within us: Something swift and tall
  Swept in and out and that was all.
  Was it a bright or a dark angel? Who can know?
  It left no mark upon the snow,
15   But suddenly it snapped the chain
   Unbarred, flung wide the door
   Which will not shut again;
And so we cannot sit here any more.
     We must arise and go:
20   The world is cold without
    And dark and hedged about
    With mystery and enmity and doubt,
    But we must go
    Though yet we do not know
25 Who called, or what marks we shall leave upon the snow.

Charlotte Mew

THE CALLS

A dismal fog-hoarse siren howls at dawn.
I watch the man it calls for, pushed and drawn
Backwards and forwards, helpless as a pawn.
     But I'm lazy, and his work's crazy.

5 Quick treble bells begin at nine o'clock,
Scuttling the schoolboy pulling up his sock,
Scaring the late girl in the inky frock.
     I must be crazy; I learn from the daisy.

Stern bells annoy the rooks and doves at ten.
10 I watch the verger close the doors, and when
I hear the organ moan the first amen,
     Sing my religion's — same as pigeons'.

A blatant bugle tears my afternoons.
Out clump the clumsy Tommies by platoons,
15 Trying to keep in step with rag-time tunes,
     But I sit still; I've done my drill.

Gongs hum and buzz like saucepan-lids at dusk,
I see a food-hog whet his gold-filled tusk
To eat less bread, and more luxurious rusk.

20 Then sometimes late at night my window bumps
From gunnery-practice, till my small heart thumps
And listens for the shell-shrieks and the crumps,
     But that's not all.

For leaning out last midnight on my sill
25 I heard the sighs of men, that have no skill
To speak of their distress, no, nor the will!
     A voice I know. And this time I must go.

Wilfred Owen

Thinking and discussion

1 Charlotte Mew's poem generates mystery and foreboding. Just what is it that
calls and creates such an impact on the hearers? Why is there such uncertainty in
the poem?

2 In Wilfred Owen's poem we know that the calls come from the men who are still
fighting in the battlefields of the First World War. When Owen wrote this poem he
was recovering from war injuries at the Craiglockhart War Hospital. The call of his
comrades still at the Front are so strong he believes he can hear them. Owen did
respond to these, returned to the Front and was killed one week before the end of
the war.

Decisions, decisions…

We'll end this section by looking at a trio of related poems.

the Road *not* Taken

Two roads diverged in a yellow wood,
And sorry I could not travel both
And be one traveller, long I stood
And looked down one as far as I could
5   To where it bent in the undergrowth;

Then took the other, as just as fair,
And having perhaps the better claim,
Because it was grassy and wanted wear;
Though as for that the passing there
10   Had worn them really about the same,

And both that morning equally lay
In leaves no step had trodden black.
Oh, I kept the first for another day!
Yet knowing how way leads on to way,
15   I doubted if I should ever come back.

I shall be telling this with a sigh
Somewhere ages and ages hence:
Two roads diverged in a wood, and I –
I took the one less travelled by,
20   And that has made all the difference.

Robert Frost

the
Introduction

They were introduced in a grave glade

And she frightened him because she was young

And thus too late. Crawly crawly

Went the twigs above their heads and beneath

5 The grass beneath their feet the larvae

Split themselves laughing. Crawly crawly

Went the cloud above the treetops reaching

For a sun that lacked the nerve to set

And he frightened her because he was old

10 And thus too early. Crawly crawly

Went the string quartet that was tuning up

In the back of the mind. You two should have met

Long since, he said, or else not now.

The string quartet in the back of the mind

15 Was all tuned up with nowhere to go.

They were introduced in a green grave.

Louis MacNeice

Buttocks

The darkness leads us away from our goals.
Fearing the stone beneath our knees
we crawl one after another, grimly holding
onto the buttocks of an incomplete stranger,
5 forming a line through the darkness,
a line of buttock-holding strangers.
There is absolutely no fondling for fun.
We inch our way forward, slowly,
straying from our path several times.
10 Occasionally an anguished cry is heard.
Someone has lost hold of a buttock.
None of us know just whose buttocks we are holding,
if they are kind, friendly, lonely, happy or sad.
Somewhere up ahead is the light at the end of the tunnel.
15 Exactly which tunnel we have all forgotten.
We have also forgotten why we are in which ever tunnel this is.
There is no room for memory or contemplation.
Immense concentration is required to keep hold
of an unknown buttock for a lifetime.

Mark Robinson

Thinking and discussion

1 All three poems are about making choices. They are also about not making choices, not making the right choices, or having our choices made for us. They are about decision-making and missing the opportunity to make these decisions.

2 Delve deep into your mind-dictionary of 'tone' words to label the varying tones of these three poems.

3 If you are completing an extended piece of writing on these three poems, be mindful of the need to make detailed annotations. A few hints:

'The Road Not Taken'

- Is there any regret about the choice made?
- Was one road definitely 'less travelled by'?
- Why did he doubt 'I should ever come back'?
- What is meant by 'Oh, I kept the first for another day!' Is there any significance in the use of the exclamation mark?

'The Introduction'

- Who are the 'they' of the poem?
- What do you think the words 'Crawly crawly' signify?
- What is the significance of the punning on the word 'grave'?
- Why do you think they are both 'frightened'?

'Buttocks'

- What does the 'darkness' and the 'tunnel' suggest?
- For what is the 'buttock' a metaphor?
- Do you think this poem is any less serious than the other two?

Examining poetry

Whenever you write about poetry for coursework or an examination you will want to be as informed and original as possible. You can be informed by applying the 'Three Ts' and by writing about the many ideas and poetical features that shape each poem's meaning. Being original is more difficult. Whilst you are encouraged to have original views and opinions, these will be influenced by the ideas and features you and other students will have noted. These ideas and features are not, however, going to be open to endless, new interpretations!

What you can strive to do is to match your informed opinions about poems with fresh and lively writing, what an experienced Principal Examiner of GCSE English Literature has called 'writing with attitude' (*see below*). There are many exam techniques that can be learned to aid success in dealing with and answering exam questions, and some of these are listed on page 118. Writing with attitude, however, is a skill that needs to be developed over time and has a value to outlive the few hours of an examination.

Here is a fuller definition of what writing with attitude means:

Answers which are vigorous, quarrelsome and dissenting will be valued more than those which inkily transport notes on techniques from one page to another. Candidates should be prepared to write with and about attitude: attitude **in** a text, attitude **of** a writer, and attitudes **to** text and writer … literature at GCSE is all about texts with attitude, displayed with attitude, to be read with attitude and taught with attitude.

So now you have it from the horse's mouth: you can vigorously argue and disagree with the exam questions and examiners! Obviously, attitude does not mean treating the exam like a punching bag, but you do not have to treat it like a temple either. Writing with attitude means remembering the 'Mantra' introduced in Chapter 2 Techniques (*see* page 47). Writing with attitude means being prepared to argue a case and explore possible meanings without feeling that there is only one answer. For example, we looked at possible interpretations of 'Life Doesn't Frighten Me' by Maya Angelou in Chapter 1 Tones (*see* page 9).

Writing with attitude

The following extracts are responses to a study of the poems in the section 'Female of the species' from Chapter 1 Tones (see pages 20–27) and are typical of the kind of writing with attitude we are exploring. The question was:

Write about two or three poems in this group which show the poets' opinions about what is wrong with the way women are treated. You should write about:

- what the poets feel strongly about

- your response to their feelings and opinions

- persuasive words and phrases they use

- similarities and differences between the views of the men and women writers.

Extracts

1 Paul Durcan is being amusing but getting across a serious message at the same time. He is being sarcastic about the woman keeping her breasts in the back garden and we know as readers that what he really wants to get across is the idea that men treat women as sex objects. However, I think the ending of the poem becomes a little silly when he talks about Australia, and refers to the woman as Miss Delia Fair, because this seems to make fun of the woman rather than concentrate on the serious message she was trying to get across. I think the tone has changed from poking fun for a serious point to trying to be funny just for the sake of it.

'The Woman Who Keeps Her Breasts in the Back Garden' by Paul Durcan

2 I love the idea of the breasts being put on a leash and walked around like dogs. This is a great send-up of men who are only interested in a women's breasts and so she puts them on this kind of comic display. I can still imagine men wondering if they were poodles or alsations!

'The Woman Who Keeps Her Breasts in the Back Garden' by Paul Durcan

3 I don't see how you can call this a poem. It has a message about the wife feeling like a berk because she continues to do the jobs expected of women, but this is more of a statement than a poem. Compared with the others in this section, it only offers one example of rhyme to make it sound like a poem and I feel there should be more development of its main idea. Paul Durcan's poem shows how you can be funny and have a serious message but it does this by telling a full story.

'Women's Liberation' by Sue May

4 This poem doesn't need to use persuasive words or phrases because it uses its shape to do the talking. The shape of the poem is like a thread being hung because of the way it reduces to one word per line and you can imagine the man clinging on but the thread breaking. I like the sarcasm of the opening stanza where the third line says he could not follow which is a very simple but powerful way of letting us know that the woman is in total control. I can relate to this and feel that a woman's strength does not have to be the same kind of strength as a man's, say physical strength, for her

to be more powerful. This is a persuasive poem because the kind of strength talked about is realistic.

'Spider Woman' by Shamshad Khan

5   On the other hand, the poems written by men are even more hard hitting and satirical than the women's poems. There is a strong similarity between Higgin's and Wallace-Crabbe's poems as they present men as mean and bullies. I was surprised to find the men's poems this strong in criticising men and in a way I think this has more power when I read them because I feel they must really mean what they say. However, you could argue that the women have had the bad experiences and their poems are therefore more realistic. Could the men just be trying to sound as if they care about the way women are treated in order to be approved by women?

'She is Not Afraid of Burglars' by Rita Ann Higgins and 'The Wife's Story' by Chris Wallace-Crabbe

6   I don't understand all of Kipling's poem but he seems to be putting women down and this might be because this is an older poem and represents an older attitude. In the last part where he says 'Must command but may not govern – shall enthral but not enslave him' he seems to suggest that women are powerful but not as powerful as men. I actually think this is a typical man's poem with so much talking in it that everything gets twisted and you can never be sure what he actually means.

'The Female of the Species' by Rudyard Kipling

Many of these responses show either a willingness to query the authors' purposes and effects (e.g. extract 1) or to query the terms of the question's bullet points (e.g. extract 4). They are also prepared to qualify answers and ask rhetorical questions within their answers (e.g. extract 5). This is a true exploration: there will not always be definite answers and it can be more honest and informed to demonstrate the process of this kind of reaction to a poem. There is not much actual analysis in these extracts, but there is a genuine attempt to show an informed and personal response by referring to specific aspects and making judgments. The attitude shown here is that the writers were thinking for themselves and were prepared to ask questions as well as to make clear decisions.

Preparing and responding

Now it is your turn to answer the same question. This is repeated opposite but with additional handwritten notes to draw your attention to the important features of the question. Whether responding to a coursework assignment or answering an exam question, it is crucial that you annotate the question itself to pick out key points.

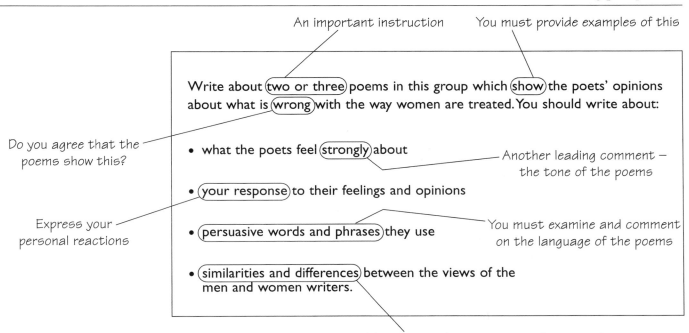

Write about (two or three) poems in this group which (show) the poets' opinions about what is (wrong) with the way women are treated. You should write about:

- what the poets feel (strongly) about
- (your response) to their feelings and opinions
- (persuasive words and phrases) they use
- (similarities and differences) between the views of the men and women writers.

An important instruction

You must provide examples of this

Do you agree that the poems show this?

Another leading comment – the tone of the poems

Express your personal reactions

You must examine and comment on the language of the poems

You must make comparisons between the poems

Thinking and writing

1 Go back to Chapter 1 Tones and re-read the poems in the section, 'The female of the species' (*see* pages 20–27).

2 Make brief notes of comparison between the poems. The following table shows an approach to making your own notes and plans. The question's bullet points may provide you with a structure, for example:

	'The Woman Who Keeps Her Breasts …'	'She is Not Afraid of Burglars'	'Spider Woman'
Strong feelings	Against treating women as sex objects	Attack on men as bullies	Celebrates the power of women over men
Persuasive words and language	The imagery of the breasts being walked: 'male-dominated society' 'bosom-gaping'	Idea that man treats wife and dog the same: 'The dog obeys him' and 'The wife obeys him' 'My husband beat him across the head/ with a whip'	Imagery of the man dangling on a thread: 'delicate construction' 'general destruction'
Similarities and differences	Uses humour to make a serious point like the Higgins poem – mainly comic	The humour is darker than in the Durcan poem – quite an angry poem	Men are not seen as strong – quite the opposite to Higgins poem. Very simple structure

3 Plan your essay. Whether writing for GCSE English or English Literature examinations you will be asked to make comparisons between poems and it is therefore important that your plan focuses on this feature. There are two possible plans for this:

  - The first, a chronological plan, is the most straightforward way to plan. Its weakness is that it is possible to lose sight of the need to make comparisons.

  - The second, a comparing plan, is slightly more complex. Its strength is that you are always focused on comparisons.

4 The notes in the table are more detailed than you would be able to reproduce in exam conditions. They are given here as a guide to the aspects you would be thinking about for either plan. Once you have read these, make a simpler plan for each model. Spend no more than ten minutes on each summary.

Chronological plan

Introduction

Answer the question. Briefly summarise your agreement or disagreement that these poems have strong opinions on the way women are treated.

First stage

Get on with the essay! Work through your first poem. Do this chronologically too.

- Show how the poet introduces the main idea/image: *Paul Durcan introduces his poem with a conversation, and the opening line (quote) suggests that the poem is going to have a comic tone.*

- Make comments on techniques and use of language. Make brief comparisons with the other poems: *Higgins' poem uses the actual conversation of the wife to make it sound realistic and this is like Durcan's poem although his dialogue is more comic.*

- Comment on use of rhyme and rhythm and any particular structure or form.

- Make brief comparisons with other poems: *the shape of 'Spider Woman' is important to the overall meaning which distinguishes it from the other poems in this section.*

Middle stage

Write about the other poems as above. You may well feel more confident in writing about one or two of the poems so deal with these first. Continue to make brief comparisons.

Final stage

Make your main comparisons here, commenting on similarities and differences. Remember to state which poem or poems you prefer and why. Be clear about why a poem is most effective for you. It may be the meaning and/or the style that you like.

Comparing plan

Introduction

This should be the same as the introduction above. The key is to address the question, state your opinion and then move into illustrating your points.

First stage

Look at the varying tones of the poems you have selected and comment on their effectiveness in conveying strong opinions. You should draw comparisons between the comic and serious tones and the similarities and differences between the male and female writers. Does the sex of the writer affect the poem's tone of voice?

Middle stage

Look at how poetic techniques and language are used.

- Two of the poems are conversational and thus the language is meant to sound authentic. Compare the effectiveness of this with the more formal language of 'The Wife's Story'. Do you have a preference when it comes to your response to their feelings and opinions?
- Look at how rhyme, rhythm and presentational/structural features work in the poems.
- Is 'Women's Liberation' a poem? How can this match the Higgins' poem for delivering a strong message?
- Discuss the sonnet form of 'The Wife's Story' and the impact of the last two lines. How does this compare with the final stanza of Higgins' poem?
- Comment on the use of para-rhyme in 'The Wife's Story'.

Final stage

State your overall preference and your response to how the poems make you reflect on their common theme.

Exam techniques

The advice that follows is largely common sense. Common sense, however, can be the first quality to desert students in the unreal hours of an actual examination. Being successful in examinations requires:

- knowledge and understanding of the subject being tested
- skills with which to explore and express this intelligently
- ability to use common-sense exam techniques such as reading questions carefully, planning work, leaving time for checking your writing, etc.

The trend in GCSE English and English Literature examinations is to have open book exams which means that students can take lightly annotated copies of their books and anthologies into the examination. The following advice is based on such an examination for poetry although it can clearly apply more generally.

Working well
in the exam

1   Make sure you have revised.

2   Make sure you bring your poetry anthologies.

3   Once in the exam room, relax and stay calm. But do not go to sleep!

4   Listen carefully to advice and instructions given by exam invigilators.

5   Read the exam paper carefully. You should already know, but note the time allocated for your answers. Throughout the exam, use time wisely. Use the clock to structure your planning, writing and checking time.

6   Read all of the relevant questions for the poems you have studied. Select the question you feel most confident in answering.

7   Annotate the question. Make sure you understand all of the specific aspects it wants you to discuss.

8   Make brief notes of comparison on the poems you are likely to use (two to three poems for a half-hour exam; three to four poems for an hour exam, whatever is requested and therefore required).

9   Make a brief plan for your answer. Think of the type of essay, chronological or comparing, and plan this in stages.

10   In an hour exam, reading and planning of 10 minutes (15 maximum) would be quite appropriate. If you can then write solidly for 35–40 minutes (leaving time to check and correct) this will be plenty of time. This is general guidance only, as individuals will differ widely in their ability to sustain solid writing. You cannot over-estimate the value of careful and considered planning. (When writing, do not over-rely on annotations in your anthologies. As well as being time-consuming, it is obvious to examiners when notes are submitted in an answer. Annotations should be brief and exist to direct you to links between poems and/or make one or two key points per poem.)

11   Check and correct. Check that you have said what you wanted to say! Be sensitive to what you have actually written not what you think you have written. Accuracy can aid the persuasive quality of your writing. Writing with attitude does not mean ignoring all the conventional features of writing!

12   Relax again. You've done your best!

Activity

The following extracts from imaginary answers require some shaping up and correcting. They represent many of the obvious but, unfortunately, typical mistakes made by students when writing about poetry, and not just in examinations! They are again based on the poems from the section 'The female of the species'. Work with a partner and try to come up with improved, ideal answers. Share these with the rest of the class and discuss the alterations:

1 The thread in 'Spider Woman' is a symbol.

2 Paul Durcan is trying to say that men treat women as sex objects.

3 The last line of 'Spider Woman' is an excellent example of enjambement. This is the only one in this poem and it isn't used by the other writers.

4 Rudyard Kipling repeats the line 'The female of the species is more deadly than the male' for effect.

5 The poem 'The Female of the Species' has a set rhyme scheme. This helps me to read it.

6 The poem 'She is Not Afraid of Burglars' is made up of eight paragraphs.

7 I found that all of these poems were very powerful in the way that they were written and they really made the reader think.

8 'The Female of the Species' lyric by Space is different from Kipling's poem because its language is very modern.

9 In both 'The Wife's Story' and 'She is Not Afraid of Burglars' there is a wife speaking and this makes them more similar than any other of the poems in this section.

10 I can understand what the message of all of these poems is but in my experience it isn't always the man who is wrong and I think that woman today go on and on about inequality but history tells us that there are differences between the sexes and it's about time we all accepted this rather than whinging on and on and on …

You will have noticed that some of the errors above were more obvious than others! The idea is that in correcting these simple mistakes you are thinking about the need always to be as focused and precise as you can when responding to examination questions and writing about poetry.

Glossary of technical terms

Alliteration	The repetition of consonant sounds in words near one another, especially when the sound occurs at the beginning of the words. The purpose is to create a particular sound effect, often to mimic the thing being described, e.g. 'Lend him to stroke these blind, blunt bullet-leads'.
Assonance	The repetition of similar vowel sounds in words near one another. The purpose is usually to create a soft sound for a particular effect, e.g. 'The milkmaids call and the tired cows yawn'.
Ballad	A narrative poem telling a story, often someone's adventure. Traditional ballads were sung by touring minstrels.
Blank verse	Unrhymed lines of verse in iambic pentameter.
Couplet	A pair of rhyming lines, e.g. 'But were some child of yours alive that time You should live twice; in it, and in my rhyme'.
Elegy	A lyric poem which is a meditation on life and death. Elegies will often mourn the death of famous people or close friends.
Enjambement	This is when the following line in a poem carries an important meaning. The following line itself can be significant because of a change in rhythm/metre or content, or the first word in the following line can draw attention to itself by being unexpected. The purpose and effect of this can be to focus the reader's attention on the following line in order to emphasise a particular point, e.g. 'To be his channel to everyone human Except a woman'.
Epic	A narrative poem that tells a lengthy story (longer than a ballad) and it is often about heroic people and their daring deeds.
Free verse	Poetry which does not follow a particular rhyming or rhythmic pattern. Seen as a more modern way of writing.
Haiku	A Japanese poetic form consisting of 17 syllables arranged in three lines: 5 syllables in the first line, 7 in the second line and 5 in the third.
Iambic pentameter	A line of ten syllables alternating between five stressed and five unstressed beats (*see* Meter).
Image	When words create a picture in the mind or appeal to our senses so that we see, hear or feel the thing being described, e.g. 'Hands are like wounds already Inside armour gloves'
Irony	This is when a writer presents a particular meaning but actually implies the opposite. Poets will often write about the irony that exists in events and situations in the world around us, e.g. at the end of the poem 'Fatima' (*see* page 17) the teacher seems caring

and concerned when asking the little girl 'Fatima, why are you crying?' Her question is ironic because it her own insensitivity that has caused the girl to cry.

Lyric	A short poem expressing a writer's feelings and emotions.
Medium	The way in which information is being communicated; for example, 'poetry' is a medium. Within poetry, rhyme or alliteration can also be described as mediums because these are particular techniques used to communicate specific sound effects. Such effects might be used to add to the overall meaning and message of a poem, e.g. the 'blind, blunt bullet leads' are harsh, alliterative sounds in a war poem about the harsh reality of dying.
Metaphor	Compares two dissimilar things in a more 'concentrated' way than a simile. One thing actually 'becomes' another. The word 'is' often signals a metaphor, e.g.

'I give you an onion.

It is a moon wrapped in brown paper.'

An extended metaphor develops its comparison and images over a whole poem as in 'The Library of Love' (*see* page 36).

Meter	The regular beat or rhythm of a line. This is determined by the stressed and unstressed sound of particular syllables. To represent this you can mark a stressed syllable with a diagonal line and an unstressed syllable with an X. The most common pattern is called the iambic meter which is an unstressed syllable followed by a stressed syllable, e.g.

$$x \quad / \quad x \quad / \quad x \quad / \quad x \quad / \quad x \quad /$$

'Their breasts were stuck all white with wreath and spray'

Narrative poetry	A poem telling a story, such as a ballad or an epic.
Octave	The first eight lines of a Petrarchan (Italian) sonnet where a particular point or idea is expressed.
Ode	A poem expressing serious feelings, often in an elaborate style.
Onomatopoeia	When a word sounds like the thing it describes. The purpose of this is to create sound effects in a poem, often to mimic and thus add reality to the thing being described, e.g. 'clip clop sandals slapped'.
Para-rhyme	(*see* Rhyme)
Persona	An assumed identity or character, usually revealed when a poet adopts the voice of a particular kind of person.
Personification	Giving human qualities to an animal, object or abstract idea, e.g.

'And the tractor, streaming with sweat,

Raging and trembling and rejoicing'.

Quatrain	A four-line stanza which normally follows a set rhyme scheme. A Shakespearean (English) sonnet contains three quatrains and a concluding rhyming couplet.
Rhyme	Words that have the same sound. The most common form of rhyme is full or perfect rhyme where the rhyming words sound exactly the same (e.g. bike/like). These also occur at the ends of lines. Alternatives to this are the use of para-rhymes where consonants rather than vowels are matched (e.g. flash/flesh), and

the use of internal rhymes where words rhyme within a line rather than the end.

Rhyme scheme	The pattern in which rhyming words occur in a poem, e.g.

A Memory

Four ducks on a pond,	a
A grass-bank beyond,	a
A blue sky of spring,	b
White clouds on the wing,	b
What a little thing	b
To remember for years –	c
To remember with tears!	c

William Allingham

Parting at Morning

Round the cape of a sudden came the sea,	a
And the sun looked over the mountains rim –	b
And straight was a path of gold for him,	b
And the need of a world of men for me.	a

Robert Browning

The rhyme scheme for the first poem is *aabbbcc*; for the second it is *abba*.

Rhythm	The beats in a line (similar to the stress of syllables as outlined in *Meter*) but can be used with much more variation. The following two lines are not matched exactly in their number of beats, but the rhythm is still perfectly clear: 　'Dis poetry is Verbal Riddim, no big words involved 　An if I hav a problem de riddim gets it solved'
Sestet	The last six lines of a Petrarchan (Italian) sonnet where the ideas expressed in the octave might be challenged, altered or reflected on in some way.
Simile	The comparison of two dissimilar things, using the words 'like' and 'as', e.g. 'Hands are like wounds already'.
Sonnet	A fourteen-line poem which establishes a point of view in one part and then reflects on or alters this in a later part.
Sound pattern	This is an overall term for the use of sound effects in a poem which help the reader to hear the things being described. It can be a combination of alliteration, onomatopoeia, assonance.
Stanza	The groups of lines within a poem.
Syllable	Each unit within a word that has a beat. Syllable has three: syl-la-ble.

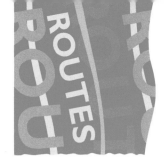

Index of poets and poems

First lines are given for untitled poems

Acknowledgements

FLEUR ADCOCK: 'Kissing' from *The Incident Room* (Oxford University Press, 1986), reprinted by permission of the author; MONIZA ALVI: 'Indian Cooking' from *The Country at My Shoulder* (Oxford University Press, 1993), by permission of the author and Bloodaxe Books; MAYA ANGELOU: 'Life Doesn't Frighten Me' from *And Still I Rise* (Virago, 1986), reprinted by permission of Little, Brown & Company (UK); SIMON ARMITAGE: 'The Catch' and 'Poem' ('And if it snowed…') from *Kid* (Faber & Faber, 1992) and 'Mice and snakes don't give me the shivers' from *Book of Matches* (Faber & Faber, 1993), reprinted by permission of the publisher; EDWARD KAMAU BRATHWAITE: 'Ogun' from *Islands* (Oxford University Press, 1969); JACQUELINE BROWN: the author for 'The Laugh' from *In a Woman's Likeness* (Arc Publications, 1996); JOHN CITIZEN: the author for 'The Library of Love' from *The Fire People: Collection of Contemporary Black British Poets*, edited by Lemn Sissay (Payback Press, 1998); JOHN COOPER CLARKE: the author for 'I wanna be yours'; E. E. CUMMINGS: 'it may not always be so;and I say' from *Complete Poems 1904–1962*, edited by George J. Firmage, © 1991 by the Trustees for the E. E. Cummings Trust and George James Firmage, reprinted by permission of W. W. Norton & Company; CAROL ANN DUFFY: 'Valentine' from *Mean Time* (Anvil Press Poetry, 1993), reprinted by permission of the publisher; HELEN DUNMORE: 'Malta' from *Short Days, Long Nights: New and Selected Poems* (Bloodaxe, 1991), reprinted by permission of the publisher; PAUL DURCAN: 'The Woman Who Keeps Her Breasts in the Back Garden' from *A Snail in My Prime* (Harvill Press, 1993), © Paul Durcan, 1993, reprinted by permission of the publisher; U. A. FANTHORPE: 'Patience Strong' from *Selected Poems* (Penguin Books, 1989), © U. A. Fanthorpe, reprinted by permission of the author; ROBERT FROST: 'The Road Not Taken' from *The Poetry of Robert Frost*, edited by Edward Connery Lathem (Jonathan Cape, 1969), reprinted by permission of Random House UK Ltd; SEAMUS HEANEY: 'Clearances. 3' from *The Haw Lantern* (Faber & Faber, 1987), reprinted by permission of the publisher; JOHN HEGLEY: 'A fisher of words' from *Five Sugars Please* (Mandarin, 1994) and 'The Firework' from *Family Pack* (Methuen, 1997), reprinted by permission of The Peters, Fraser & Dunlop Group Ltd on behalf of the author; RITA ANN HIGGINS: 'Almost Communication' and 'She Is Not Afraid of Burglars' from *Sunny Side Plucked: New and Selected Poems* (Bloodaxe, 1996), reprinted by permission of the publisher; TED HUGHES: 'Tractor' from *Moortown* (Faber & Faber, 1979), reprinted by permission of the publisher; PAT INGOLDSBY: 'For Rita With Love' from *Salty Water* (The O'Brien Press, 1988), reprinted by permission of the publisher; LINTON KWESI JOHNSON: 'Reggae Sounds' from *Tings an Times: Selected Poems* (Bloodaxe Books, 1991), reprinted by permission of the publisher; TIMOTHY EMLYN JONES: the author for 'pass' from *Grandchildren of Albion* (New Departures, 1992); SHAMSHAD KHAN: the author for 'Spider Woman' from *The Fire People: Collection of Contemporary Black British Poets*, edited by Lemn Sissay (Payback Press, 1998); RUDYARD KIPLING: 'The Female of the Species' from *Selected Poems* (Penguin Twentieth Century Classics, 1993), reprinted by permission of A. P. Watt Ltd on behalf of The National Trust for Places of Historic or Natural Beauty; PHILIP LARKIN: 'XXIV' from *The North Ship* (Faber & Faber, 1974), reprinted by permission of the publisher; GERALD LOCKLIN: the author for 'my son wants to ride the chairlift' and 'what I learned from watching the pink panther cartoon festival' from *The Firebird Poems* (Event Horizon Press, 1992), © 1992 Gerald Locklin; EILEEN McAULEY: the author for 'The Seduction'; SUE MAY: 'Women's Liberation' from *Frankenstein's Daughter* (Stride Publications); IAN McDONALD: the author for 'Decorated For A Kiss' from *Caribbean Poetry Now* (Hodder & Stoughton, 1984); ROGER McGOUGH: 'Waving at Trains' from *Selected Poems* (Jonathan Cape, 1989), reprinted by permission of The Peters, Fraser & Dunlop Group Ltd on behalf of the author; LOUIS MacNEICE: 'The Introduction' from *The Collected Poems of Louis MacNeice* (Faber & Faber, 1979), reprinted by permission of David Higham Associates Ltd; GLYN MAXWELL: 'The Perfect Match', excerpted from 'Short Lyrics' and 'Poem in blank rhyme' from *Out of the Rain* (Bloodaxe Books, 1992), reprinted by permission of the publisher; ADRIAN MITCHELL: 'The One About Fred Astaire' from *Blue Coffee: Poems 1985–1996* (Bloodaxe Books, 1996), reprinted by permission of The Peters, Fraser & Dunlop Group Ltd on behalf of the author. Educational Health Warning! Adrian Mitchell asks that none of his poems are used in connection with any examinations whatsoever; WILFRED OWEN: 'The Calls' from *The Complete Poems of Wilfred Owen and Fragments*, edited by Jon Stallworthy (Chatto & Windus, 1983), reprinted by permission of The Estate of Wilfred Owen and Random House UK Ltd; MARIO PETRUCCI: 'Latitude' from *Shrapnel and Sheets* (Headland Publications, 1996); SYLVIA PLATH: 'Blackberrying' from *Crossing the Water* (Faber & Faber, 1975) and 'Metaphor' from *Collected Poems*, edited by Ted Hughes (Faber & Faber, 1981), reprinted by permission of the publisher; CRAIG RAINE: 'A Martian Sends a Postcard Home' from *A Martian Sends a Postcard Home* (Oxford University Press, 1979), reprinted by permission of David Godwin Associates on behalf of the author; MARK ROBINSON: 'Buttocks' from *The House Burning Park* (Stride Publications, 1994); ROGER ROBINSON: the author for 'The Last Dance' from *The Fire People: Collection of Contemporary Black British Poets*, edited by Lemn Sissay (Payback Press, 1998); ANN ROUSE: 'England Nil' from *Sunset Grill* (Bloodaxe Books, 1993), reprinted by permission of the publisher; SIEGFRIED SASSOON: 'Base Details' from *Collected Poems 1908–1956* (Faber & Faber, 1961), copyright Siegfried Sassoon, reprinted by kind permission of George Sassoon; CAROLE SATYAMURTI: the author for 'Between the Lines' from *Broken Moon* (Oxford University Press, 1987) and 'Fatima' from *Striking Distance* (Oxford University Press, 1994); RUTH SILCOCK: 'The Buddha's Wife' from *Mrs Carmichael* (Anvil Press Poetry, 1987), reprinted by permission of the publisher; SPACE: 'The Female of the Species' (Gut Music/Hit & Run Publishing); ANDREI VOZNESENSKY: Darhansoff & Verrill Literary Agency on behalf of Stanley Kunitz for 'First Ice' by Andrei Voznesensky, translated by Stanley Kunitz (Basic Books); CHRIS WALLACE-CRABBE: 'The Wife's Story' from *Selected Poems 1956–94* (Oxford University Press, 1995); JUDITH WRIGHT: 'Age to Youth' from *Collected Poems* (Carcanet Press, 1994), reprinted by permission of HarperCollins Publishers Australia; BENJAMIN ZEPHANIAH: 'Dis Poetry' from *City Psalms* (Bloodaxe Books, 1992), reprinted by permission of the publisher.

The publishers would be pleased to rectify any omissions or errors brought to their notice at the earliest opportunity.